The Life and Times of
GEORGE III

The Life and Times of
GEORGE III

John Clarke

Introduction by Antonia Fraser

Weidenfeld and Nicolson
5 Winsley Street London W1

© George Weidenfeld and Nicolson Limited
and Book Club Associates 1972

Series design by Paul Watkins
Layout by Rodney Josey

Filmset by Keyspools Ltd, Lancashire
Printed in Great Britain by
C. Tinling & Co. Ltd, London and Prescot

Contents

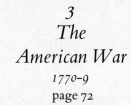
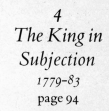

Introduction

THE SIXTY-YEAR REIGN of George III constitutes the longest span of all our Kings, and in British history is beaten only by that of his granddaughter, Queen Victoria. George III came to the throne in 1760, a pleasing young man of twenty-two, described by Horace Walpole (no sycophant where Royalty was concerned) as 'his person tall and full of dignity, his countenance florid and good natured, his manner graceful and obliging …'. He died in 1820 at the age of eighty-two, having lived out the last ten years of his life in total madness, and now blind as well, a decrepit old man with a few sparse white hairs on his head, and only the Star of the Garter, which he kept obstinately pinned to his dressing-gown, to show that he was still, in theory at least, King of Great Britain. The contrast between the two Englands which George found on his accession and left behind him after his obscure unmourned death was equally profound if less dramatic: for within that period had occurred not only the startling loss of the American colonies, but also, geographically nearer home, the French Revolution with its climacteric effect on political opinion in England as in the rest of Europe.

Between the enduring importance of the events over which he presided, and the tragic ending to his life, the true personal character of George III has been too little regarded. It is easy to wash over the humiliating mishandling of America as due to the incompetence of George and his ministers – although the Americans themselves acquitted George in the years leading up to Independence – while his descent into lunacy in old age has often given rise to the quite unjustifiable assumption that George spent much of the rest of his reign as a 'contemptible idiot'. The endless fascinating manipulations of the domestic politics of the era should not distract us from the nature of the King himself, who emerges from John Clarke's moving and illuminating biography as an essentially sympathetic and in some ways even saintly man.

In this rehabilitation of George III – a monarch who, quite unlike his Hanoverian forbears, loved England and was nicknamed Farmer George for his appreciation of the beauties of the countryside – the reassessment of the nature of his malady naturally plays a part. It is helpful to realise that he was actually suffering the purely physical effects of porphyria, a recently-discovered disease of the pigmentation, and that there is therefore no need to search his youthful behaviour for signs of psychological unbalance. In fact, until the ultimate madness of 1810, less than one year of his reign had been spent in madness. All the more is one's heart wrung by the appallingly cruel medical treatment the King had forced upon him by the mercenary and power-mad royal doctors, with the connivance of his wife and eldest son, who as Prince Regent was almost as unfilial as Lear's daughters.

But personal tragedy apart, the examination of the record shows that for twenty years at least, and intermittently thereafter, George III displayed many excellent and honourable qualities of the type most desirable in a sovereign, including hard work in application to his royal duties and courage and resolution in a crisis such as the Gordon Riots. His simple domestic life with Queen Charlotte and their numerous progeny might be unimpressive at first to subjects more used to royal debauchery, but as the reign proceeded, his strongly-held religious faith, combined with his own evident probity provided a much-needed stabilising influence in an age of European chaos; while his private interest, whether botany, prison reform or Sunday schools, were all in some way aimed at enhancing the quality of English life. It would be a pity if an unfortunate genetic fluke which destined George III to end his days in unhappy darkness, also prevented us from appreciating a King who, as John Clarke puts it, believed steadfastly in 'the honour of England and its Crown' – two admirable values for any monarch.

Antonia Fraser

Acknowledgments

Photographs and illustrations are supplied by, or reproduced by kind permission of the following. The pictures on pages *2*, 10–11, 13/1, *14–15*, 17, 18–19, 26, 31, 62, *68*, *80*, 94, 95, 106, 114–5, 119, 129, *146–7*, 154–5, *158–9*, 182, 183, 198, 203, 213 are reproduced by gracious permission of H.M. the Queen; on page 40 by permission of Viscount Boyne; and on page 137 by courtesy of the Archbishop of Canterbury (copyright reserved by the Courtauld Institute of Art and the Church Commissioners). Batsford Limited: 126–7/1; British Museum: 13/2, 16, 20, 24, 34–5, 39, 43, 44, 46, 55, 78–9, 79, 83/1, 83/2, 86, 89, 90, 92–3, 96, 100–1, 111, 118/1, 118/2, 121, 130–1, 133, 140–1/1, 143/1, 143/2, 164, 165, *177/1*, *177/2*, 191, 208; Commander Campbell-Johnson, Brighton: 63; Courtauld Institute: 137, 139; Department of the Environment (Crown Copyright): *3*, 60–1; William Gordon-Davis: 163; A.F. Kersting: 126–7/2; Lambeth Palace: 137; City Art Gallery, Manchester: 97/2; Mansell Collection: 22, 23, 54, 54–5, 150–1, 160, 164–5, 186–7, 209; National Maritime Museum: 202; National Monuments Record: 124, 127; National Portrait Gallery: 50, 59, *65/1*, *65/2*, 73, 77, 102, 123, 174–5, 181, 195; Radio Times Hulton Picture Library: 21, 75/1, 75/2, 104–5, 128, 140, 140–1/2, 142–3, 157, 167, 169/1, 169/2, 171; Royal Academy: 40, 97/1, 107; Royal College of Physicians: 132; Science Museum: 50–1, 51, 84/1, 84/2, 85; Rodney Todd-White: 143/1, 143/2; Victoria and Albert Museum: 161, *180*; 188/1, 188/2, *189/1*, *189/2*, *189/3*, *192*; Josiah Wedgwood & Sons Ltd: 152.

Picture research by Jane Dorner.

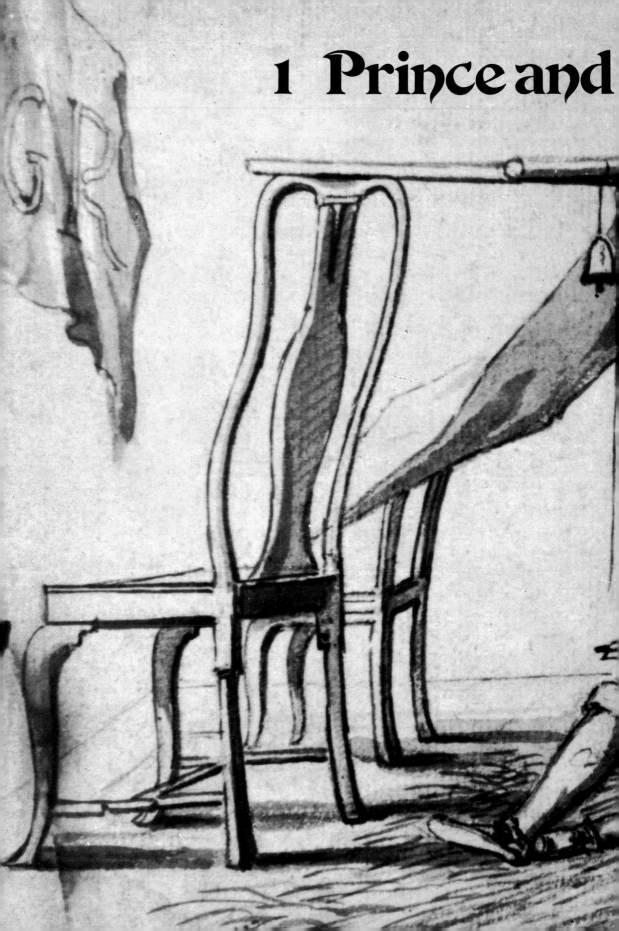

GEORGE WILLIAM FREDERICK, eldest son of Frederick Prince of Wales and Augusta of Saxe-Gotha, was born at Norfolk House, St James's Square, London, at 7.30 am on 4 June 1738. It was a premature birth; Augusta was taken in labour so unexpectedly that only one officer of State – Dr Potter, the Archbishop of Canterbury – arrived in time for the delivery. The child seemed weak and was not expected to live, but survive it did and by its very existence became an important factor in politics. The circumstance of the royal birth reflected an important feature of the Hanoverian dynasty – the perennial hostility between the Sovereign and his heir. Prince George was born at Norfolk House because his grandfather, George II, had ordered Frederick out of St James's Palace. Later the family moved to Leicester House, Leicester Square; the Square became known as 'the pouting place for princes'.

Personal differences were sharpened by the encouragement given to the Prince of Wales by politicians opposed to the King's ministers. Such men hoped that when their protégé came to the throne he would dismiss their enemies and install themselves in power. Prince Frederick was unpromising material for this tactic. As Duke of Cornwall, the Prince of Wales wielded considerable political influence in the West Country, but he lacked the persistence to produce results of real importance and seems to have been a weak character. Lord Hervey wrote:

> His behaviour was something that gained one's good wishes, though it gave one no esteem for him. For his best qualities, whilst they prepossessed one the most in his favour, always gave one a degree of contempt for him at the same time. His carriage, whilst it seemed engaging to those who did not examine it, appeared mean to those who did ... he had a father that abhorred him, a mother that despised and neglected him, a sister that betrayed him, a brother set up to pique, and a set of servants that neither were of use to him nor desirous of being so.

It is hard to imagine that Frederick would have made a good King; he was one of nature's failures. He was rather like an overgrown child, happiest when with his children and writing short plays for them to perform. He was superstitious and made frequent visits to fortune tellers in Norwood Forest. Although he cultivated pretty women, many believed that Frederick was impotent. Miss Anne Vane was being rather condescending

PREVIOUS PAGES Drawing of George as a child, playing soldiers in a tent constructed by flags over chairs.

OPPOSITE ABOVE Frederick, Prince of Wales, at the gaming table, one of his favourite pastimes. Drawing by Hogarth. BELOW Leicester Square in the mid-eighteenth century. Leicester House – the London home of Frederick, Prince of Wales – is the fore-courted building just right of centre.

LEICESTER SQUARE

when she described the Prince of Wales 'in these matters ignorant to a degree inconceivable but not impotent and as capable of having children as any man in England'. Frederick anticipated many of the failings of his grandson, the future Prince Regent but, unlike George IV, he was never to face serious responsibility. 'Poor Fred' died on 20 March 1751, aged forty-eight.

Frederick's death made an enormous difference to his son George who was created Prince of Wales a month before his thirteenth birthday. George II was sixty-seven and a new reign could not be far away. Hitherto, the boy had led a sheltered life, he was young for his years and had a poor grasp of reading and writing. Now, his education became a political question. The 1750s were the greatest days of the Pelham family headed by the Duke of Newcastle. The Pelhams and their relations had such influence in government that they came to think they had a right to power. They saw themselves as the Guardians of the Revolution of 1688, the heirs of the men who had deposed the Catholic despot James II and replaced him with the Protestant William of Orange. Because of this signal service, the country owed them a perpetual debt. George II had long accepted the domination of the Pelham clique, but it was vital for them to secure the heir to the throne. It was the Duke of Newcastle, rather than the King, who chose Lord Harcourt as the Prince of Wales's governor.

Unfortunately for the Pelhams, Harcourt neglected his duties and the task of forming Prince George's mind fell to his sub-governor, Andrew Stone. It was not long before Stone was accused of infecting the Prince with arbitrary principles. In panic, Harcourt claimed that Stone was a Jacobite who made his pupil read *Histoire des Révolutions d' Angleterre* by Père d'Orléans – a book expressly written to defend James II's unconstitutional measures. Stone was also charged with introducing his pupil to Bolingbroke's *Patriot King*. This asserted the King's right to choose his ministers where he would and portrayed him as the natural protector of the people against exploitation by the aristocracy. As George was an obedient boy who believed what he was told, the Pelhams were horrified at the implications for the future.

It is unlikely that the wretched Andrew Stone thought he was

PREVIOUS PAGES Frederick, Prince of Wales and his family at Park Place, Henley, in about 1743. Four of the royal children, including Prince George, are shown seated in a chariot decorated with the royal arms and the Prince of Wales's feathers: painting by John Wotton.

RIGHT Frederick, Prince of Wales – 'Poor Fred' – who died in March 1751. Portrait by Highmore.

BELOW Title page of *Histoire des Révolutions d'Angleterre*, by Le Père d'Orléans, one of the Jacobite books given to the Prince of Wales by his sub-governor, Andrew Stone.

HISTOIRE
DES
REVOLUTION
D'ANGLETER
Depuis le commencement de la Mor
jusqu'au Regne de Guillaume II

PAR LE PERE D'ORLE
De la Compagnie de JESUS.

TOME PREMIE

Nouvelle Edition, corrigée & enrichie de Cart
Portraits des Rois de la Grande Bretagne

A LA HAYE,
Chez RUTGERT ALBERTS, L
MDCCXXIII.

introducing an unacceptable theory, George I and George II
would have had little difficulty in accepting a definition of the
sovereign's function similar to that advanced by Bolingbroke.
The Glorious Revolution and the Hanoverian Succession were
designed to make England safe for Protestantism, not to reduce
the King to the same level as the Doge of Venice. In fact, no
additional legislative restrictions were placed on royal power

Augusta, Princess of Wales
wearing a black veil to
show her recent widow-
hood, sitting with her
children. In the background
hangs a portrait of the
deceased Prince in his robes
of State. On the left of the

between 1714 and 1760, but there was a difference between theory and practice. Neither George I nor George II could speak English fluently; both spent much of their time in Germany, and George II, in particular, wanted a quiet life. The result was that royal power had been gradually eroded. With a determined young man on the throne, things might be very different.

Stone's influence on George was small compared to the power exercised by his mother. Augusta was a stronger character than her husband. She was a devoted and domineering mother who dragooned her son to accept a rigid, essentially German, attitude to religion and a crushing sense of duty. Augusta was ambitious, and her ideas of monarchy were decidedly absolutist – she had caused something of a sensation by hurling herself full length on the floor when first presented to George II. Lord Hervey described her as:

> Rather tall and had health enough in her face, joined to a very modest and good-natured look, to make her countenance not disagreeable but her person was, from being very ill-made, a good deal awry, her arms long and her motions awkward, had, in spite of all the finery of jewels and brocade, an ordinary air which no trapping could cover or exalt.

Augusta took no part in politics while her husband was still alive; she had only to wait and she would be Queen of England. In 1751 the Princess of Wales was only thirty-two and had no intention of withdrawing into the modest seclusion of widowhood. She expected to exercise power through her son, and in this task she was helped by her friend – and probably more than friend – the Earl of Bute. According to Lord Chesterfield, the Prince saw hardly anyone except his mother, Bute and personal servants, so that Bute came to have a very great influence over him. To the awkward young boy, he seemed the complete man of the world whose advice, company and friendship were eminently desirable.

George II had never liked his daughter-in-law; according to some reports, he believed that an alliance with the House of Saxe-Gotha would bring 'evil and insanity' into the Royal Family. Hereditary defects were indeed present, but the danger was greater in the King's own family than in his daughter-in-law's. George II wanted to free his grandson from Augusta's

group is George, Prince of Wales, showing a plan of the fortifications of Portsmouth to his brother, Edward, Duke of York (in military uniform). Painted in 1751 by George Knapton.

Pit Ticket

THE COCK-PIT ROYAL.

apron strings. In 1755 when George was seventeen, the King found a young woman whom he believed would make an admirable bride for the Prince of Wales. The girl was the eldest daughter of the Duke of Brunswick-Wolfenbuttel. Augusta was a jealous and possessive mother who dreaded the loss of her son. If George had to marry, she planned to advance an impoverished and appropriately grateful young woman from her own family. Such a frightened creature would defer to her mother-in-law in all things.

Augusta persuaded George that, notwithstanding flattering pictures, the Princess of Brunswick was a hideous monster. The young man was terrified at the idea of being *bewolfenbuttled,* and the project had to be given up. Further attempts to separate George from his mother by giving him his own apartments in St James's Palace were not well received. He insisted that Bute should be the head of his household. Nothing at all had been achieved.

George was a 'mother's boy' and his deep-rooted puritanism

William Hogarth brilliantly portrayed the brutality and depravity of London life in the mid-eighteenth century. OPPOSITE Gin Lane, St Giles in 1751. At this period, gin could be sold anywhere and is shown being dispensed from a shed. ABOVE The Cock-Pit Royal in Birdcage Walk, St James's Park. The characters shown here are drawn from all walks of life, including a Frenchman wearing the Order of St Louis.

21

Quakers at a meeting in London. The sect had religious objections to the taking of any oaths. They thus experienced difficulties in testifying before courts of law and could not become borough councillors or members of Parliament.

was appalled by the brazen advances of young women who wanted to be the Prince of Wales's first mistress. He was too sensitive not to be repelled by women who were obviously more attracted to his position than to himself. Beneath the priggish exterior, however, George was developing an interest in women. Because of his secluded upbringing, he was all the more liable to make a fool of himself over a girl he really fell in love with.

This was to be Hannah Lightfoot, the daughter of a Quaker tradesman, from Execution Dock, Wapping-in-the-East. It was not a salubrious area; its rotting, disease-ridden courtyards cannot have been very different from those described in horrifying detail by Henry Mayhew one hundred years later. In the 1750s the parish was a centre of cock-fighting and bouts between female prize-fighters. The main occupations were lighterage, street trading, petty thieving and prostitution. The industry, cleanliness and sobriety of the Quakers may have raised the Lightfoots a little above their neighbours. Later in the century, Quakerism was regarded as a rich man's religion, well-represented in great brewing dynasties like the Barclays; in the 1750s it was still a poor man's belief, scarcely tolerated by the law. Neither the area nor the sect seemed likely to produce a woman

22

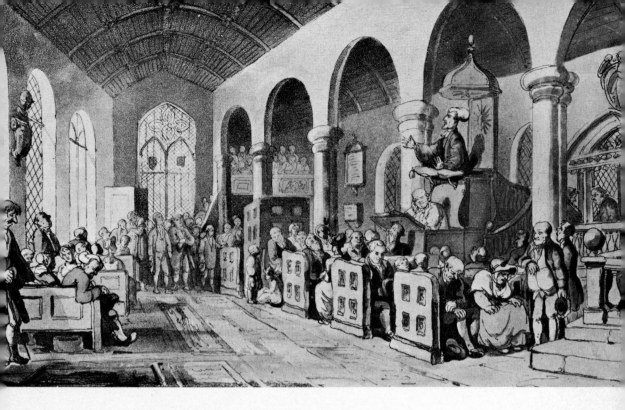

believed by some to be the rightful Queen of England.

Miss Lightfoot had an uncle who was a successful linen draper in the West End. Early in 1754 Hannah was staying at the draper's home on the corner of Carlton Street and St Albans Place. In the arch words of a nineteenth-century biographer, the house was 'interesting perhaps as having been the last in which she was destined to press the pillow of innocence'. Leicester House was not far away and somehow or other Hannah met the Prince of Wales. She was not, however, at all eager to become George's mistress. The contrast between her background and attitudes and those of the hard and elegant ladies of the Court could not have been more striking. Her attraction for the shy young man to whom grandeur meant loneliness is easy to appreciate.

Hannah's virtue only increased George's infatuation. In the end Miss Chadleigh, who acted as a go-between for the Prince, managed to fill the girl's head with visions of magnificence and break down her remaining scruples. According to Hannah's family, she was married off to a Mr Axford but continued to be visited by the Prince by whom she had several children. So far as is known, Hannah never attempted to exploit her position and lived the remainder of her life in obscurity.

Dr Syntax preaching, an engraving by Rowlandson, showing Sunday service in an Anglican church. The congregation had to pay for the privilege of a seat in the pews and the sermons were frequently long and boring.

23

Cartoon showing George as Prince of Wales, courting the fair Quakeress, Hannah Lightfoot.

If this is the whole story, it is just a repetition of the fate of so many women who have taken royal lovers. Some people – mostly cranks it must be admitted – have asserted that Hannah was not George's mistress but his wife. *A Secret History of the Court of England* by Lady Anne Hamilton claims that the wedding took place sometime in 1759 at the Curzon Street Chapel, Mayfair, in the presence of George's younger brother, the Duke of York. Lady Hamilton believed that Queen Charlotte discovered her husband's secret in 1765 and insisted on another ceremony between herself and the King. The book points to George's guilty conscience over his bigamy as the real cause of his future madness.

The present Royal Marriages Act invalidates any union involving a member of the Royal Family who has not first obtained the Sovereign's consent. The Act dates from 1772 and thus if George *did* marry Hannah Lightfoot, on his accession she was the rightful Queen and Charlotte's children, including the future George IV and William IV, were illegitimate. George was in love with Hannah Lightfoot and bore the scars of the rela-

24

tionship for some time, but this does not substantiate Lady Hamilton's allegations. The Prince had too keen a sense of duty to his family and to the country to commit the incredible folly of marrying a Quakeress from Execution Dock.

George meanwhile sought escape from personal problems by asking for employment in the army. George II, who was the last English King to lead his troops into battle – at Dettingen in 1743 – misconstrued his grandson's letter as a demand to be made Commander-in-Chief in the event of a French invasion. The old warrior King was determined to keep that position for himself. But Prince George had not long to wait. His grandfather's hearing and eyesight were failing; it seemed to the King that everyone's face was covered with black crepe.

Like his son Frederick, George II died suddenly – at breakfast time on 25 October 1760, and the next day Prince George was proclaimed King. Unlike George II, who had destroyed his father's will, George III respected his grandfather's wishes. His private feelings about the late King were none too warm but, with the new Sovereign, personal inclinations took second place to duty. A Mr Clavering, a groom of the Bedchamber who refused to sit up at night with the corpse, was instantly dismissed. It was a king's mistress who normally lost most by his death. At one moment she was surrounded by flatterers; the next, she had no status at all. In most instances she would now be mocked by her enemies and driven from Court in disgrace. If her protector made provision for her, his successor often found a pretext to appropriate the legacy for himself. Lady Yarmouth fared better than most of her kind. Six thousand pounds in bank notes was found in George II's desk with a request that the money should go to her. George III not only complied but added another two thousand guineas.

The King's good intentions were universally acknowledged. Even the Pelhams thought all would be well. The Duke of Newcastle declared that George had done everything to assist the ministers inherited from his grandfather. Horace Walpole, not usually sympathetic to royalty, wrote:

> His person is tall and full of dignity, his countenance florid and good natured, his manner graceful and obliging. ... I saw him yesterday and was surprised to find the levée had lost so entirely the air of the lion's den. The Sovereign does not stand in one spot with his

eyes fixed royally on the ground, and dropping bits of German news. He walks about and speaks freely to everybody. I saw him afterwards on the throne, where he is graceful, sits with dignity and reads his answers to addresses very well.

George was twenty-two and seems to have possessed every advantage. Although not outstandingly handsome, the young King was generally regarded as good-looking in a rather Germanic way. His face, and in particular his prominent eyes, already gave some indication of his strong character. He was the first monarch since Queen Anne to have been born and educated in England. His grandfather and great-grandfather had made themselves unpopular by their obvious preference for Hanover, and had been constantly threatened by the claims of the House of Stuart. Now Charles Edward Stuart was no longer the dashing hero of the '45, but an ageing debauchee whose followers were looking for an excuse to transfer their allegiance to the House of Hanover. The country was prosperous and in recent years several new colonies had been acquired. The war with France was going well and 1759 had probably been the most successful year in the whole history of British arms.

Although Newcastle had given his approval, it was soon evident that their new King was going to challenge the existing structure of power. When Newcastle had his first audience, the King told him 'My Lord Bute is your good friend; he will tell you my thoughts.' When the Privy Council met, Newcastle was asked to deliver a ready prepared speech on the King's behalf. There was nothing remarkable about the speech except its authors. George II's speeches had usually been written by Newcastle or by one of his secretaries; this was prepared by the King and Bute. Several members of the Privy Council, including the great Pitt, were astonished at the young man's presumption.

In many ways, Newcastle was a ridiculous man. His behaviour at George II's funeral was disgraceful in a First Minister of the Crown. On entering Henry VII's Chapel in Westminster Abbey, he burst into hysterical sobs, flung himself into a stall and had to be revived by the Archbishop of Canterbury who had had the good sense to bring a bottle of smelling salts. A few minutes later, Newcastle got up and dashed about peering

OPPOSITE George as Prince of Wales in 1759; portrait by Sir Joshua Reynolds.

27

through his eye-glass to see who was there. For the remainder of the service, he insisted on standing on the Duke of Cumberland's velvet train because he was frightened of catching a chill from the bare stone floor. If the eighteenth century was the Age of Elegance, it was never the Age of Decorum.

Newcastle and the Pelhams had glaring faults, but still the country was indebted to them. The good prospects for the new reign were partly the result of their work. They knew a good man when they saw one, and their alliance with Pitt the Elder had given the country an outstanding war leader. Above all, they were English; the Dowager Princess of Wales was German and Bute a Scotsman. The influential classes, aristocracy, the sons of rich merchants and even country squires might go on the Grand Tour but fundamentally they were xenophobic. Their distrust of foreigners included Scots as well as Germans. The area euphemistically known as 'North Britain' had been united with England for less than sixty years; its inhabitants were either feared as Jacobites or resented as grasping savages who had stolen colonial trade which properly belonged to England. The idea that the Court favourite should be a Scotsman, as in the days of James I, was quite intolerable.

George III was too trusting, a terrible failing in a monarch. His mother told him that his own capacity was limited and that he should trust Bute who had remarkable talents; he believed her. His lack of contact with the outside world meant that he had no yardstick against which to measure these assertions. The Pelhams were selfish and grasping, but some of their professed anxiety was genuine. It was not long before ministers were giving discreet encouragement to popular feeling against Bute and his supposed mistress. The slogans 'No Petticoat Government' and 'No Scotch favourite' were painted on the walls of the Royal Exchange. Augusta was driven from theatres by obscenities screamed from the galleries. One day when the King went to visit his mother, a voice from the crowd asked him whether 'he was going to suck'. Despite the good opinions, the new King would be in serious trouble if he allowed his mother and Bute to have too much influence.

Although George continued to obey his mother on political matters, a serious threat appeared to her emotional hold over the King – Lady Sarah Lennox. Sarah was poison to any possessive mother. She was seventeen, beautiful, fascinating and a flirt with several admirers at her feet. She was, moreover, the daughter of the Duke of Richmond and a direct descendant of Charles II. Unlike poor Hannah Lightfoot, she was of sufficient social standing to have a real hope of becoming Queen. Augusta could not contain her jealousy and publicly insulted the girl, but if she had lost control over her son's affections, her political influence might not last much longer. Her anger was shared by Bute; the King was pliable and, if he married Sarah, he would fall into the hands of the Lennox family and their ambitious relation, Henry Fox.

The King appeared besotted. Most mornings in the spring of 1761, he rode to Holland House to meet his love. In the grounds he would find Lady Sarah, advantageously dressed in what was supposed to be peasant costume. The pastoral idyll, so beloved of the world-weary aristocracy, seemed ready for transformation into the medieval splendour of a coronation in Westminster Abbey, with Sarah at George's side as Queen. It was not to be. Augusta's pleas, recognition of the difficulties inherent in a marriage between King and subject and knowledge of Sarah's dalliance with Lord Newbottle forced the King to give up his suit. Augusta had proved her hegemony in battle with another woman. The King would obey her in all things, but she had to act quickly before he could consider returning to Sarah.

Reluctantly, George despatched a Colonel Graham to report on foreign princesses. The Sovereign was compelled by law to marry a Protestant; he was also Elector of Hanover and therefore political considerations made it likely that his bride would be German like his mother. Graham's choice fell on Sophia Charlotte, youngest daughter of the Duke of Mecklenburg-Strelitz. The King's mother made her own enquiries and decided that this young woman was not a threat in the way Sarah Lennox had been.

The betrothal was announced on 8 July 1761. Few people in England had ever heard of the small North German principality of Mecklenburg-Strelitz. Strelitz, which is now part of East Germany, was rather a squalid town. The unkind suggested that the country would be better described as 'Muckleberg Strawlitter'. Even in polite society it was said that the main difficulty now would be in finding the bride's dominions. As far as Augusta was concerned, there were advantages in an alliance with a slightly comic-opera German dukedom. Despite their royal blood, Charlotte's family would have been regarded as paupers by many an English peer. At home, the eighteen-year-old-girl had only one proper gown which was kept for Sunday wear. She would probably feel nervous in her exalted position and was unlikely to take any political initiatives of her own.

Mr Drummond, the English ambassador to Prussia, went to Strelitz to perform the betrothal ceremony. After dinner, the Princess was laid on a sofa upon which Drummond placed his foot – this strange custom seems to have been a watered-down version of the practice general in the sixteenth century, when the girl was then put to bed in the presence of her family whilst her suitor's ambassador put his leg, stripped to the knee, between the sheets as a token of consummation.

Charlotte professed proper astonishment and alarm at the position she was called to, but any qualms were overcome by lavish presents of jewels. She was put in the care of the Duchess of Ancaster, the Duchess of Hamilton and the Countess of Effingham and conveyed from Cuxhaven to England in a boat renamed the *Charlotte*. Various opinions have been expressed about Queen Charlotte; Lady Anne Hamilton described her as 'one of the most selfish, vindictive and tyrannical women that ever disgraced human nature'. This is unfair; whatever may have happened later, in 1761 Charlotte seems to have been a pleasant and vivacious girl. Although she had attractive dark hair and a good complexion, she was hardly a beauty – short, thin and pale with a prominent nose and large mouth. She would have had to have been a saint to emerge unembittered from the trials of the next few years.

The *Charlotte* was expected to sail up the Thames to be met by the King at Greenwich, but bad weather forced the Princess to land at Harwich and continue the journey by road. The bride was well received by the London crowds and seemed happy enough until she came to St James's Palace, which she thought forbidding. It was there that George first saw her; according to some observers he had difficulty in concealing his disappointment.

About ten o'clock the same evening – 8 September 1761 –

The storm which befell Queen Charlotte's passage to England in September 1761 forced her to land at Harwich. The scene is dramatically depicted in this painting by Wright.

Charlotte proceeded to the Chapel Royal with the King's brothers, the Duke of York and Prince William, at her side. She was dressed in white and silver, with a train of violet velvet lined with ermine fastened to her shoulder by enormous pearls. It was sumptuous but very uncomfortable and Charlotte can scarcely have looked her best. Her train and tiara were so heavy that she could not stand upright. Lady Sarah Lennox was a bridesmaid and looked much prettier. It cannot have pleased Charlotte when the aged Earl of Westmorland had to be forcibly restrained from doing homage to Sarah as Queen of England.

31

After the marriage ceremony, the company returned to the
Drawing Room and inconsiderately stayed until four in the
morning. At last, George could be alone with his wife, but even
then some of the guests resented Charlotte's refusal to follow
the ancient custom of admitting the company into the royal
bed-chamber.

A fortnight later, George and his Queen were crowned.
During the ceremony, the King gained good opinions by
removing his crown when receiving the Sacrament. Special
efforts were made for the coronation banquet held in Westminster Hall. The Hall was in darkness until the Queen arrived,
but then a thousand lights suddenly transformed the scene.
Spectacles of this sort were dangerous, for the lamps were lit
almost simultaneously by putting tapers to waxed strings which
hung from one lantern to the next. For a minute or so the company was showered with burning wax. The risk was worth it.
The sudden illumination of men on horseback, gold plate,
peers in velvet and ermine, judges in scarlet, ladies covered in
jewels, bishops in vestments and the splendid liveries of the
pursuivants and heralds must have been a breath-taking sight.

By eighteenth-century standards, the banquet was well
organised. There were a few trifling incidents. The Sword of
State had been forgotten and the Lord Mayor's had to be borrowed instead. The Lord High Steward, Lord Talbot, had to
enter on horseback, ride up to the dais, make obeisance and then
back his horse out of the Hall. Great efforts had been made to
teach the animal to walk backwards when leaving the Banquet.
Unfortunately, the horse had learnt only too well and insisted
on entering backwards and advancing towards the King and
Queen rump first. More seriously, one of the largest jewels fell
out of the crown; twenty years later when England lost her
American colonies, there were some who recalled this omen.

At the end of the Banquet, the King's Champion, Lord Errol,
issued a challenge to anyone who disputed his master's right to
the throne. This was probably the last coronation when any one
imagined that the Champion would actually have to fight.
Many people, including the historian David Hume, believed
that the Stuart Pretender had slipped into England and was
standing in the public galleries of Westminster Hall. Perhaps
Charles Edward had considered taking up the challenge as a last

gesture to a doomed cause. If so, the Pretender changed his mind; according to one source he told a man who recognised him 'the person who is the object of all this pomp and magnificence is the person I envy the Least'. George could afford to ignore any remaining Jacobite threat; in a brief moment of sanity at the end of his life, the King paid for a monument in St Peter's, Rome to the memory of the Stuart claimant.

The first year of George's marriage was not happy. Augusta made Charlotte's life miserable. She was determined to crush any signs of independence and dominate the Queen as much as she did her son. When she discovered that the Duchess of Mecklenburg had asked her daughter not to wear jewels when taking communion, the Princess of Wales demanded that she should. One of Charlotte's relaxations was playing cards with her maids; soon all games of chance were prohibited as wicked. Things might have been more tolerable had not George usually sided with his mother against his wife. The King's unmarried sisters mocked Charlotte's lack of sophistication, but every effort was made to prevent her making English friends. English ladies were forbidden even to approach her without first obtaining permission from her German attendants. Charlotte had difficulty in keeping order amongst her servants and was actually faced with a strike of maids. Lack of discipline brought tragedy. One girl thought that things were so chaotic that no one would notice if she stole a few of her mistress's jewels. She was caught and sentenced to death. Charlotte intervened and managed to have the sentence reduced to slavery in the American plantations.

It was not an auspicious beginning. The Royal Family was shut up in Buckingham House and rarely appeared in public. Augusta increased her campaign and recruited Miss Katherine Dashwood to spy on the Queen. Charlotte's treatment may help to explain her behaviour to her own daughter-in-law many years later. The Court was dull and getting duller. Such was the economy imposed by Lord Talbot, that the King and Queen usually dined off tough mutton and inferior claret. George's good nature gave place to coldness and melancholy. For a few weeks he was ill with pains in his limbs and stomach, but he soon recovered and was cheered by the birth of a son, the future George IV, on 12 August 1762.

'The person who is the object of all this pomp and magnificence is the person I envy the Least'

2 Learning the Hard Way 1762-70

Augusta thought the time had come to implement her plans to install her favourite in power. Bute had once been a whist companion of Prince Frederick. He was a handsome man and the symmetry of his legs in their tight-fitting stockings is said to have won Augusta's heart. Bute's manner, however, was not that of a successful womaniser; in fact, he was extremely pompous. He was a discriminating patron of the arts, but his political talents were limited. Frederick's judgment had been damning – 'Bute would make an excellent ambassador in a Court where there is no business.' He was not the best man to take on the political establishment.

Fortunately for Augusta, the government's unity was precarious. Ministers considered themselves directly responsible to the King and had little sense of loyalty to the Prime Minister. George and his mother had room for manœuvre. Bute was believed to be naïve and professional politicians thought they could use him to their advantage against their colleagues, so that no one objected when Bute replaced the Earl of Holderness as Secretary of State.

The next step was more serious. When Pitt demanded hostilities against Spain, he found himself in a minority and was forced to resign. He was extremely popular amongst the ordinary people, especially in London. On a royal visit to the City on 9 November 1761, he received a tumultuous welcome whilst Bute was in danger of being savaged by the mob. At dinner in the Guildhall, the King drank to the health of the Corporation of London, but the toast was received in dead silence.

Pitt's departure reduced the government's majority in Parliament and its authority in the country, but it was safe so long as it was backed by the Pelham connexion. But Newcastle had to be driven from office if there was to be a clean sweep and the government given a new tone. Although George constantly insulted the Duke, Newcastle seemed prepared to put up with anything. The malicious Horace Walpole declared that with the dregs of life he clung to the dregs of power. Newcastle finally resigned on 26 May 1762. George was not a man to kick an enemy when he was down. The Pelhams' fortune had been much reduced by their enormous political expenses and the King proposed to give the retiring Prime Minister a pension

PREVIOUS PAGES Cartoon of 1763 by Hogarth, with a statue of George III in the centre and 'Butefying' London in the background.

36

corresponding to his long services. The offer was refused.

With Newcastle out of the way, Bute became Premier. It seemed that the Crown had broken out of the strait jacket restricting it for so long. However, it was one thing to put Bute into office and another to keep him there. The new Premier might have the King's favour but could he gain Parliament's? The monarch was so closely identified with his minister that, if Bute fell, George's own reputation would suffer. George and Bute wanted peace with France, and the Duke of Bedford soon obtained apparently favourable terms. Parliament was still in a bellicose mood, Pitt and the Pelhams were united in opposition and Bute was no more popular. The government was insecure but a majority had to be obtained somehow. Bute recruited Henry Fox, who had learned the art of Parliamentary 'management' from Newcastle, to do what he could. The King and Augusta despised Fox as corrupt and unprincipled but in order to ensure their victory over the Whig grandees they had to employ the very methods they objected to in others. George wrote sadly 'we must call in bad men to govern bad men'. It is the perennial dilemma of the idealist in politics.

'We must call in bad men to govern bad men'

Some of Fox's friends, notably the Duke of Devonshire, were expected to joined the government. When the Duke refused, he was dismissed as Lord Chamberlain and George took the unusual step of personally erasing his name from the list of Privy Councillors. Retribution fell on those who had been appointed by the Pelhams: lords lieutenant were dismissed, tellers of the Exchequer replaced, and a poor man in Sussex who had distinguished himself in a battle with armed smugglers lost his pension because it had been obtained for him by the Duke of Grafton. There was even more corruption than under the previous government. £25,000 was spent on bribery in one morning and traffic in votes in Parliament became so open that members assembled outside the Paymaster General's office to receive their 'wages'.

On the best estimates, slightly less than half the members of Parliament were bribable – even if funds had been available to deal with the remainder. There were standards; many members would accept a present to reinforce their support for a cause they already believed in, but they would not vote against their conscience. The independent country gentlemen, the real core

37

of the Lower House, were tied to no particular party and considered it their duty to support 'the King's government' unless there was overwhelming reason to do otherwise. Their outlook was rather old-fashioned, their notion of the Constitution included a powerful Crown and they expected the King to choose his own Ministers. They were surprised when George chose Bute, a man outside the circle of established faction leaders, but they were ready to give the new government a fair trial.

The main issue was peace with France. The war may have been in the interest of the grandees who expected grants of land in captured territories; it may have been in the interests of merchants who made profitable contracts with the armed forces and looked forward to new trading preserves in an enlarged Empire; patriotic fury was never far from the surface of the London mob. To the country gentlemen, men in the mould of Fielding's Squire Western, the war was less attractive. They were unlikely to derive any special benefit if hostilities continued to Doomsday – to them war only meant increased taxation. They would never consent to sell England short, but they would favour an honourable peace. George III was young and politically naïve but he had one great advantage: despite his German parentage, his outlook and prejudices coincided with those of most country squires. He knew almost instinctively what the country gentlemen would take and what they would not. This quality helps to explain many of the King's successes in the future.

Parliament met on 25 November 1762. When the great Pitt appeared, scarcely capable of walking, his legs wrapped in flannel, his face pained and emaciated, the government knew that its task would be difficult. Pitt spoke against the Peace for three and a half hours. Walpole wrote, 'he had the appearance of a man determined to die in that cause and at that hour'. Despite these herculean labours, the Peace Preliminaries were approved by three hundred and nineteen votes to sixty-five.

The Court was in seventh heaven, the old Cabal was defeated and Augusta could say 'Now my son *is* King of England.' For the moment the Whig magnates made no further attempts to resist, but Bute's triumph was short-lived. Peace was the most defensible aspect of his policy; now other parts came under scrutiny. He was accused of planning a personal despotism. In a

RIGHT Scurrilous verses satirising the relationship between Bute and Princess Augusta.

GISBAL, LORD OF HEBRON.

Ld Bute.

THE
STAFF of GISBAL:

An Hyperborean SONG,

Translated from the Fragments of OSSIAN, the Son of FINGAL.

By a YOUNG LADY.

" *Arma virumque cano.*" VIRGIL.

N. B. This SONG is a fuitable Companion to the Book of GISBAL.

I.

YE frolickfome Laffes in Country and City,
    Attend for a while to a frolickfome Ditty!
Thou Spirit of OSSIAN, great Son of FINGAL,
Affift me to fing of the STAFF of GISBAL!
Derry down, &c.

II.

When this notable Chief of the HEBRONITES Land
Before BATHSHEBA ftood, with his STAFF in his Hand,
The Damfels around her cry'd out, one and all,
" What a *wonderful* STAFF is the STAFF of GISBAL" !
Derry down, &c.

III.

From the Days of old ADAM there has not been found,
Thro' the World's ample Circuit, a STAFF fo renown'd:
Not the CHEROKEE KING, or NABOB of BENGAL,
Can boaft fuch a STAFF as the STAFF of GISBAL.
Derry down, &c.

IV.

If Madame Pompadour had this Prodigy feen,
She'd have own'd it was fit for the Ufe of a Queen;
And that LOUIS LE GRAND, with his BATON ROYAL,
Was lefs *magnifique* than the STAFF of GISBAL.
Derry down, &c.

V.

Of fuch exquifite Virtue this STAFF is poffeft,
It will kindle Emotions of Love in your Breaft:
For a proof of this Truth, I appeal to them all,
Who have ever beheld the fam'd STAFF of GISBAL.
Derry down, &c.

VI.

No STAFF ever made of *Gold, Silver,* or *Wood,*
Could compare with this Compound of pure *Flefh* and *Blood:*
A STAFF fo upright, I may venture to call,
A STAFF for a PRINCESS — this STAFF of GISBAL.
Derry down, &c.

VII.

Entomb'd with his Fathers when GISBAL lies rotten,
Though worn to a *Stump,* it fhall ne'er be forgotten:
As a *Trophy* we'll bear it to WESTMINSTER HALL,
And hang up the *Remains* of the STAFF of GISBAL.
Derry down, &c.

VIII.

If Critics fhould cenfure, or Witlings fhould laugh,
And fay " furely MISS ftands in Need of a STAFF,"
I defy the moft fwaggering Blade of them all,
To produce fuch a STAFF as the STAFF of GISBAL.
Derry down, &c.

LONDON: Printed for the AUTHOR, and Sold by the Bookfellers and Print-fellers.
[Price Six Pence.]

cartoon entitled 'The Royal Dupe' the King was pictured sleeping in his mother's lap whilst Bute stole his sceptre and Fox picked his pocket. A scurrilous 'underground' press existed throughout the eighteenth century and had to be accepted as a fact of life. Now there was a new dimension; Lord Temple, a member of the previous Cabinet, was in direct communication with the publishers of the most obscene attacks. The Whig grandees considered themselves amongst the first gentlemen of Europe, but when dealing with an upstart Scotchman, they were completely unscrupulous. The London mob responded and the Prime Minister did not dare to go out without disguising himself.

Bute was not the only unpopular Minister. As a young man Sir Francis Dashwood, the Chancellor of the Exchequer, had been a member of the Hell-Fire Club, which dabbled in the occult and claimed to practise black magic. One Good Friday, Dashwood was in Rome and slipped in amongst the penitents in the Sistine Chapel. The candles had been put out and the congregation prepared to beat themselves with the small scourges distributed by an attendant. Suddenly Dashwood leapt up brandishing a cutting-whip and proceeded to lash out in all directions. The penitents experienced more pain than they had bargained for and the future Chancellor of the Exchequer escaped amidst screams of '*Il diavolo! Il diavolo!*' Dashwood's unpopularity was not due to this unfortunate affray in the Vatican but to his financial mismanagement. His muddled budget was received with derision but his proposal to tax cider provoked fury against the government amongst the very group of country gentlemen who had been so useful in the previous session. In the cider counties, effigies of Bute, clad in tartan and decorated with the Order of the Garter, were paraded about leading a donkey representing the King.

Bute resigned suddenly on 8 April 1763; Fox and Dashwood left office with him. The great families were reorganising their forces and the Prime Minister lacked the courage to withstand a prolonged attack. George's eldest sister, the Duchess of Brunswick, believed that Bute resigned so that the King would beg him to stay in office. If so, he was disappointed. George III was now twenty-four and could not be kept in cotton wool for ever. His outlook was broadening and he could see that Bute was

OPPOSITE Sir Francis Dashwood at his mock devotions. Dashwood was notorious for his part in the activities of the Hell-Fire Club and his interest in black magic. Portrait by Hogarth.

making the Crown unpopular. The lesson that 'mother is always right' had to be unlearned. Having emancipated himself from the Whig grandees, George's next problem was to find a satisfactory alternative.

At first it seemed that George Grenville, Secretary of State in Bute's government, was the answer. The King had a Germanic faith in 'experts'; he thought that a man who had the minutiae of government at his finger tips would make a good Prime Minister, regardless of his other qualities. Grenville worked hard, his personal life was blameless, he knew all the Parliamentary precedents and seemed to thrive on complicated columns of figures. Once, when the new Prime Minister fainted in Parliament and smelling salts were administered, George Selwyn was heard to say, 'Why don't you give him the Journals to smell too?' Unfortunately, Grenville's bad qualities outweighed the good. He was arrogant, obstinate and utterly tactless. His efforts to tax the Americans provoked the first serious discontent across the Atlantic.

In the short run, Grenville's greatest mistake was his attack on John Wilkes, the member for Aylesbury. Wilkes played an important part in securing the rights of the individual, but personally he was a spendthrift libertine and a member of Dashwood's dubious circle. In the early 1760s Wilkes was trying to recoup his losses by turning to rabble-rousing politics. The racy wit of his paper *The North Briton* (a dig at Bute) soon made him famous. A fortnight after Grenville took office, No. 45 of *The North Briton* accused the government of deceiving the country, although its tone was mild compared to earlier attacks on Bute. Grenville could have continued his predecessor's policy of ignoring Wilkes, or he could have offered the author of *The North Briton* a lucrative job and thus converted him into one of the administration's most fervent admirers.

Instead, the Prime Minister decided to gag Wilkes – regardless of the danger of turning a scoundrel into a popular martyr. Wilkes and forty-nine of his associates were arrested on 29 April 1763 under a General Warrant which, without specifying names or supposed crimes, allowed men to be arrested and their property searched. General Warrants were not actually illegal but there was an understanding that they should be used only in times of acute national danger. Grenville had no time for under-

OPPOSITE John Wilkes, the rabble-rousing member for Middlesex. Etching by Hogarth.

Issue No. 45 of *The North Briton*, in which John Wilkes accused Grenville and his administration of deceiving the country.

N° XLV.* Saturday, APRIL 23, 1763.

The following advertisement appeared in all the papers on the 13th of April.

THE NORTH BRITON makes his appeal to the good sense, and to the candour of the ENGLISH nation. In the present unsettled and fluctuating state of the *administration*, he is really fearful of falling into involuntary errors, and he does not wish to mislead. All his reasonings have been built on the strong foundation of *facts*; and he is not yet informed of the whole interiour state of government with such *minute precision*, as now to venture the submitting his crude ideas of the present political crisis to the discerning and impartial public. The SCOTTISH minister has indeed *retired*. Is HIS influence at an end? or does HE still govern by the † *three* wretched tools of his power, who, to their indelible infamy, have supported the most odious of his measures, the late ignominious *Peace*, and the wicked extension of the arbitrary mode of *Excise?*

   * The passages included within the inverted commas are the *only* passages, to which any objection is made in the INFORMATION filed in the *King's-Bench* by the *Attorney General* against the publisher, Mr. *George Kearsly*.

   † The earls of *Egremont* and *Halifax*, and *G. Grenville*, Esq;

standings and was ready to use any device within the letter of the law to stifle those who opposed him. After a few days in the Tower, Wilkes obtained a writ of *Habeas Corpus* and was brought before Mr Justice Pratt. Pratt said nothing about General Warrants but ruled that, as a member of Parliament, Wilkes was exempt from arrest for libel. The episode brought yet more odium to the Crown.

Having used Bute and Grenville to break the Whig grandees, George thought he could deal with his own protégés much as he pleased; he would try any number of ministers until he found the man he wanted. Drastic changes were necessary, but the grandees seemed to control the best political talents. There was no question of reinstating the group *en masse* but the King hoped that, having been taught a lesson, individual members would take office on his terms.

George opened negotiations with Pitt. After a preliminary interview with Bute, Pitt was summoned to Buckingham House and had the satisfaction of forcing the Prime Minister to wait in an ante-chamber for two hours whilst he was talking to the King. When Grenville was received, he told the King what he thought of his conduct in no uncertain terms, until George abruptly terminated the audience. Unfortunately, Pitt's terms were harsh; he demanded the reinstatement of the whole of the Whig group and the dismissal of everyone who had voted for peace with France. The King could not accept this; he replied 'Should I consent to these demands of yours, Mr Pitt, there would be nothing left for me to do but to take the Crown from my own head and place it upon yours and then patiently submit my neck to the block.' George was in a difficult position. He had upset his Ministers and failed to come to terms with the Opposition, and the mistake meant loss of dignity. At one stage he even spoke of giving up the Crown and retiring to Hanover. At least the Whigs had been more courteous to the King than his present Premier.

For the moment, there was no alternative to Grenville, and Minister could dictate to Monarch as much as in the great days of the Pelhams. Grenville shared the Whigs' hatred of Bute and would only continue in office if the Earl was banished from London. This done, the Prime Minister was able to recruit the Duke of Bedford into his government. Pitt's demands were

Buckingham House, the mansion in St James's Park which became the London home of the Queen in 1762.

generally regarded as excessive and the government enjoyed modest popularity. Grenville spoilt his strengthened position by launching a new attack on Wilkes, this time because of an obscene and blasphemous poem entitled *An Essay on Woman*. The author of *The North Briton* had decided to leave England, but first he successfully prosecuted Robert Wood, an Under Secretary of State, for the illegal seizure of his papers. £1,000 damages were awarded and Lord Cambden ruled that General Warrants were illegal. The device was capable of extension into completely arbitrary arrest; in that sense the tremendous popular enthusiasm for Wilkes was not misplaced. Grenville secured Wilkes's expulsion from Parliament and the miscreant retired to France. For the moment it seemed that the campaign had succeeded, but neither the government nor the King had heard the last of John Wilkes.

Although George had made mistakes, this inexperienced young man was growing up fast. Men of affairs had to admit they had underestimated him. He seemed nervous and tended to speak far too rapidly but, underneath, he had great courage and

46

resolution. He was ready to work hard and undertake the grinding daily business of going through mounds of despatch boxes – few monarchs have been so conscientious. Reading despatches was not a glamorous occupation, but it did mean that after three or four years George had more experience of official business than the politicians who came in and out of office. To some extent, at least, knowledge was power.

After recovering from his illness in 1762, the King continued his secluded way of life. Parliament gave the Queen Richmond Lodge – built by Lord Ormonde in 1704 and granted by George I to the Prince of Wales, later George II, in 1722. The Queen's London residence was Protector Somerset's palace in the Strand which had been used as the jointure house of the queens of England since the beginning of the seventeenth century, but this was now exchanged for Buckingham House, a brick-built mansion in St James's Park. The house was small compared to Buckingham Palace, which occupies the site today, but George III found it large enough and used it as his main London residence. It was at Buckingham House, often called the Queen's House, that Charlotte gave birth in 1763 to her second son, Frederick, later to be Duke of York.

In later times the simplicity of the King's domestic life might have increased his popularity, but in 1763 it was expected that a monarch should live in the grand manner. George was supposed to be mean and rumours that the Queen's hairdresser doubled up as a waiter did nothing to change this impression. In fact, the King was not niggardly and could be very generous. When Lady Molesworth and three of her daughters died in a fire which destroyed their house in Grosvenor Square, George paid for a house for the surviving children. Between confinements the Queen was busy. In the early days of their marriage, she and George had spoken in French or German but now she had to devote a good deal of time to learning English properly. She succeeded so well that before long she spoke the language better than most members of the Royal Family and almost without trace of a foreign accent. Although she loved jewellery, Charlotte was fundamentally a prude whose influence in preparing the country for 'Victorian' respectability was considerable. The Queen gave generously to societies devoted to the reform of prostitutes; her attitudes caused first amusement and then resentment amongst the ladies whose upbringing in the England of George II had been less strait-laced than the standards prevailing at the Court of Mecklenburg-Strelitz.

Grenville was planning, meanwhile, to tax the American colonies for the benefit of the British government: he could discover nothing in law to prevent the scheme and that was good enough for him. On 10 March 1764 he announced his plan to impose Stamp Duties on the American colonies. The revenue produced would be small – £40,000 at most – but protests from the Provincial Assemblies were ignored. In Parliament, few appreciated the significance of Grenville's proposals and the Stamp Act was passed after what Burke described as one of the most languid debates he could remember.

The precise authority of the Imperial Parliament over the colonies had never been defined. In the past, British policy had been one of 'salutary neglect'. When the Duke of Newcastle left office, there was a whole room full of unread American despatches. No one seemed any the worse. The eventual separation of England from her rapidly expanding colonies was probably inevitable, but it happened much earlier than any reasonable person would have predicted in 1760. In 1763 the Treaty of Paris gave Canada to Britain; this meant that the French threat to New England and New York was removed. These colonies no longer needed British military protection and felt able to fend for themselves. Under the circumstances it was foolish to impose an entirely unprecedented tax, however light.

On 12 January 1765 the King was taken ill with what appeared to be a heavy cold. He was feverish and complained of 'stitches' in the chest. He was seen by Sir William Duncan who ordered the patient to be bled. Fourteen ounces were taken from a vein in the foot; the treatment was repeated several times in the following weeks but with no success. By the beginning of March the King's pulse-rate was 120, his face contorted and occasionally his manner was thought peculiar.

Although alarmists feared for George's reason, there is no evidence that he was actually insane. His doctors were unanimous in attributing his agitation to 'evil humours' rising from other parts of the body and affecting the brain. It was an utterly medieval theory of medicine, but at least the doctors were right

'My mind is ulcered by the treatment it meets from all around'

48

in their belief that any peculiarity in the King's mental state was to be explained by his physical illness.

The illness had serious implications. The King's life was precarious, his heir was only two years old but the law was extremely vague as to what should be done in the event of a minority. There was no obvious person to choose as Regent and, in order to avoid friction in the family, the King wanted to nominate someone known only to himself. The danger was that the King might nominate his mother. Several ministers believed that the recovery was only temporary and that George was dying of an incurable 'consumption'. The question was urgent; if Augusta became Regent, Bute would return to power. Grenville was determined to prevent this at all costs, and he sent Lords Halifax and Sandwich to explain to the King that his mother was so unpopular that Parliament would insist on her exclusion. Under the circumstances, her dignity would suffer less if George simply proclaimed her disqualified from the Regency. The King reluctantly accepted their advice.

Time had reduced but not destroyed Augusta's influence over her son. The King began to have second thoughts. He realised that Grenville was deceitfully exploiting the Crown for his own ends. It was not at all certain that Parliament would insist on Augusta's exclusion. The Prime Minister was simply taking a short cut to guarantee that he would remain in power if the King died. Ministers had become so unpopular that members might have taken up Augusta's cause. One should never be taken in by professions of undying hostility, especially from office-hungry men like the Newcastle Whigs. The eighteenth century is full of unlikely coalitions and most leading politicians would have agreed to make the Devil Foreign Secretary in their next government if they thought that they would take one step nearer power. George's acceptance of Halifax's arguments closed the issue but, by their deception, the existing Ministers, 'King's Friends' as they called themselves, had proved that they were even less concerned with the real interests of the Crown than Newcastle had been. Grenville's behaviour soon became common gossip, there was a general reaction in Augusta's favour and ministers thought it wise to reinstate her as a possible Regent. The Prime Minister developed a persecution mania. The harangues in which he denounced all of George's personal

Industrial Revolution: Textiles

In the mid-eighteenth century, James Hargreaves, a carpenter from Blackburn, invented the Spinning Jenny to spin thread. However the thread thus produced could be used only as weft because it lacked the firmness necessary in warp. It was Richard Arkwright, a former barber from Preston, who supplied this deficiency by inventing the spinning frame, thus making possible large-scale manufacture of thread. Arkwright and two associates set up a factory at Crumford in Derbyshire in 1771. He then worked on further machines to improve the processes of carding, roving and spinning.

LEFT Portrait of Sir Richard Arkwright, painted by Joseph Wright of Derby.

ABOVE Arkwright carding engine, which was used to untangle the fibres before spinning. This engine dates from the 1770s.

RIGHT Spitalfields hand loom, used by the silk weavers of East London in about 1810. This machine has a jacquard to control the warp threads.

friends grew steadily longer and more offensive. The King told Bute, 'When he has wearied me for two hours, he looks at his watch to see if he may not tire me for an hour more.'

The government was no more popular with the people. George was alarmed by the popular discontent which Grenville seemed incapable either of suppressing or of appeasing. After a powerful speech by the Duke of Bedford, a bill to improve wages and working conditions for Spitalfield weavers was rejected by the House of Lords on 13 May 1765. The next day four thousand weavers marched out to Wimbledon where the King was reviewing troops. George listened to their grievances and the marchers returned to London. On 15 May the Spitalfield men surrounded Parliament carrying red and black flags; the Duke of Bedford was hit by cobblestones as he left the House of Lords. Conditions deteriorated and for two days London was given over to mob rule. One hundred and thirty-six soldiers were needed to guard Bedford House and still the rioters almost managed to force their way in. The red and black flag was hoisted alongside the Royal Standard at the House of Lords, armourers' shops were looted and Horace Walpole thought the ordinary people were on the edge of a general insurrection. The first half of the eighteenth century had been a relatively prosperous time for the working man; falling food prices and a drop in the rate of population growth improved his bargaining position and the purchasing power of his wages. Now that population growth was picking up and a run of bad harvests producing high prices, the working classes were feeling the pinch. They might have been unable to analyse the cause of their distress, but their mood of anger and destruction was very similar to that felt by the people of Paris a few years later. Fortunately for the propertied classes, the King did not lose his nerve – always the fatal step. More troops were brought to London and gradually things returned to normal.

George had to get rid of Grenville, and Pitt appeared the only man capable of restoring the Crown's popularity. The Great Commoner was interested, but his brother-in-law, Lord Temple, the fomenter of riots, friend of Wilkes and elder brother of Grenville, had other ideas. The Wilkes affair had estranged Temple from Grenville but the two had come together over the Regency Question. Now Temple saw the possibility of a Grenville-Temple-Pitt combination to dominate the King in a way which even the Pelhams would have envied. If this plan was to succeed, it was vital that Pitt should not be detached by a separate initiative from the Crown.

Pitt was more influenced by Temple than by the King. For the second time George had antagonised one set of Ministers before securing the services of their successors. He had to go back to Grenville certain that the Premier would be more insolent than ever. Ministers met on 21 May 1765 to decide on their conditions when asked to return – compared to this, George II had been a free man. The next day the King had to face the dreaded interview. Grenville rebuked George for his ingratitude when the Prime Minister had 'sacrificed hitherto every consideration of interest, pleasure and happiness, nay of health too, to my willingness and desire to serve your Majesty' – Queen Victoria was not the first monarch to be spoken to like a public meeting. Grenville enjoyed keeping the King in suspense and would give no reply to his request to stay in office. At 9.15 pm George sent a message begging for an answer, but it was not until midnight that Grenville announced that he would return – but only on condition that Bute and his brother were permanently excluded from public affairs, that Lord Holland (the former Henry Fox) should be dismissed as Paymaster of the Forces, and that Lord Granby should be made Commander-in-Chief.

Grenville was back in office but no one believed that he had George's confidence. At levées, the King smiled at the Premier's enemies and scowled at his friends. While George recognised that Grenville worked hard, he was right in thinking that all was not well. In some departments there had been 'slackness, inability, precipitation and neglect'. Further, there could be no pretence at unity among members of the government; the only thing they had in common was their taste for laying down the law to the King. When Grenville was staying at his country house in Buckinghamshire in June 1765, George's daily lecture on his ingratitude and duplicity was left to the Duke of Bedford. Bedford took matters further than Grenville and calmly threatened the King that if he made any difficulties for the government, Ministers would accuse Lord Bute of treason, secure his conviction by the House of Lords and bring him to

Industrial Revolution: Canals

Francis Egerton, 3rd Duke of Bridgewater, has been described as the originator of British inland navigation. He was a leading member of London Society, but, following a broken engagement, decided to retire to his estates and to devote himself to the making of canals. His first venture was the creation of the canal from Manchester to Worsley to transport coal from his estates. The construction of this major undertaking was carried out by James Brindley, the famous engineer. In 1762 Bridgewater obtained Parliamentary powers to provide an improved waterway between Liverpool and Manchester by means of a canal, and this was completed ten years later.

ABOVE Stourport, on the Staffordshire and Worcestershire Canal.
LEFT Brindley's aqueduct over the River Irwell, which formed part of the canal between Worsley and Manchester.
RIGHT Engraving by H. Cook of the Duke of Bridgewater, with Brindley's famous aqueduct in the background.

the block. George declared that if he had not broken into a heavy sweat, his indignation would have suffocated him. With less provocation, George II had been known to behave in a most unkingly way by putting his boot to the offending minister and kicking him from the room.

It was third time lucky for the King. Pitt would not take office without Temple and the only way out was to negotiate with the Newcastle Whigs. The Marquess of Rockingham agreed to become Prime Minister with Newcastle as an *éminence grise* Lord Privy Seal. Until the last moment, Grenville believed that George could not do without him. Rather than admit their dismissal had been caused by their own overbearing conduct, Ministers tried to blame the Princess Dowager and her sinister influence. George Selwyn said they reminded him of criminals on their way to the gallows who blamed bad women for their ruin.

The wheel had come full circle. The Whigs, who had been the King's keepers, now seemed his liberators. The Rockingham ministry, however, was only a shadow of the Whig ascendancy of the 1750s. The party had degenerated into factions and Rockingham would be opposed by Grenville, Temple and probably Pitt. Charles Townsend thought the government 'a mere lute string administration, pretty summer wear but it will never stand the winter'. The Whig group was not strong in Parliamentary talent but it had great advantages of birth and fortune; it included members of a confident governing class, an aristocracy which had done well out of enclosures and saw no reason to prevent it profiting from the urban property market and from exploitation of mineral wealth lying beneath its estates.

The government's most serious problem was discontent in America. Attempts to enforce the Stamp Act produced denunciations of George III's 'tyranny'. There was rioting in several cities and customs houses were burned. Soon a boycott of British goods was organised and American debtors seized the opportunity to repudiate loans due to British merchants. There were bankruptcies in Bristol and Liverpool, and the Stamp Act became almost equally unpopular on both sides of the Atlantic.

Ministers had to decide whether to repeal a recent Act of Parliament; if they did so it would be taken as a sign to the people of Britain that any unpopular legislation could be over-thrown by taking to the streets. Grenville was all for enforcing the law – at bayonet point if necessary – but Rockingham decided to repeal the Stamp Act while maintaining Parliament's abstract right to tax the colonies. A 'Declaratory Act' was passed with little protest and the repeal of the Stamp Duties approved by 275 votes to 167. The decision greatly enhanced the Ministry's standing in the eyes of the merchant community.

The King's position was equivocal. He thought that the Stamp Act should be retained on the Statute Book, but modified to render it less objectionable to the colonists. If the only alternative to repeal was to collect the tax by force, then George genuinely preferred to see the duties abolished. His position was impractical, but there is no evidence to support allegations that he was so attached to the Stamp Act that he secretly encouraged members of Parliament to vote against the government. George disliked Rockingham's attempts to pander to popular opinion, but at least he was an improvement on Grenville. The King declared that he would rather meet the former Premier 'at the end of my sword than let him into my closet'. Bute was still accused of influencing the King's mind but Rockingham was satisfied that George had kept his word to have nothing to do with the former favourite. The King wrote to congratulate the Prime Minister on his success in repealing the Stamp Duties while Rockingham did not complain of the Household officials who voted with Grenville.

In the meantime, Temple, Bedford and Grenville had concluded an alliance against the new government. They enlisted George's brother, the Duke of York, tried to contact the Queen and even made overtures to Bute. The Earl could have his revenge. Bedford and Grenville implored his forgiveness and said they had never been serious in their threats of impeachment and execution. Bute was unmoved and refused to have anything to do with them. Attempts to obtain an audience with the King were unsuccessful and when the repeal of the Stamp Act finally received Royal Assent, Grenville commented acidly 'It is clear that both England and America are now to be governed by the mob.'

'It is clear that both England and America are now to be governed by the mob'

Rockingham followed the repeal of the Stamp Act by legisla-

57

tion which forbade the issue of General Warrants. The King shared some of Grenville's fears. Today, popularity is the main goal of most politicians, but in the eighteenth century it was feared that the country's long-term interests would suffer in the rush to obtain short-term credit with the people. It was admitted that the leading merchants and financiers of the City of London were people who mattered, but Rockingham seemed to be making a wider appeal by his measure on General Warrants. George's fears may have been undemocratic but there is a difference between an informed electorate and an illiterate mob easily swayed by tub-thumping orators. The 'lumpenproletariat' mob was a factor in London politics, but Rockingham's appeal was not to this group, but to the lower middle class of shopkeepers, craftsmen and small merchants. Although few of this class could vote in Parliamentary elections, they were influential in the Livery Companies and thus in the attitude of the City Corporation. The City had been opposed to the Court and the government for the previous fifty years and, as the Wilkes case demonstrated, the tension could have serious consequences. Rockingham was certainly wise in trying to bridge the gulf.

Rockingham was only George's second choice. The man he really wanted was Pitt. The King had never believed that Pitt was sincere in his denunciations of royal power; no one could rival the Great Commoner in his following amongst the ordinary people. If George could but 'hook' Pitt it seemed that all would be well. Rockingham offered Pitt a subordinate position in his government but his terms were contemptuously rejected. Soon afterwards, the Lord Chancellor, Lord Northington, decided that Pitt's return to power was inevitable; he went to the King and told him that Pitt would probably be more tractable now that he was having second thoughts about his alliance with Grenville. Pitt had been high-handed in the past but now his language was appropriately respectful. Professional politicians may have despised the young King but, with the exception of Grenville, they hid their true feelings. Pitt knew that it was the business of politicians in office to defer to the King – or at least appear to. It was their best security of tenure. The man who had talked about conditions a few months earlier now said he wished he could 'change infirmity into wings of expedi-

OPPOSITE William Pitt the Elder, 1st Earl of Chatham; painted in about 1754 at the studio of W. Hoare.

tion, the sooner to have the high honour of laying the poor but sincere offering of my little services at your Majesty's feet'. George was so pleased to have secured Pitt that he was extremely curt to the outgoing ministers. Rockingham was angry with the King for ejecting him so unceremoniously; it was a resentment which was to have serious consequences in later years.

Rockingham followed his predecessors and found Lord Bute a convenient scapegoat to explain his dismissal. According to Temple's spies, Bute never went near the King during the critical days, although he continued to have surreptitious meetings with the Princess Dowager at Miss Vansittart's house in Sackville Street. The employment of spies seems to have been general. Lord Rockingham retained one of George's personal servants and another reported frequently to the Duke of Richmond. Some attempts were made to reinstate Bute in George's favour. Without knowing that Bute would be staying there, the King accepted an invitation to visit his aunt, Princess Amelia, at her house near Brentford. As soon as he saw Bute, the King turned his back and reproved his aunt for her foolish experiment.

In fact Bute could not matter much unless George was still dominated by his mother. The King now saw little of Augusta; in her last years she devoted her oppressive mother's love to her younger son, the Duke of Gloucester, until she died in 1772. In these years few members of the Royal Family had time for political intrigue. Charlotte had a child almost every year; William, Duke of Clarence, Edward, Duke of Kent, Ernest, Duke of Cumberland, Augustus, Duke of Sussex, Adolphus, Duke of Cambridge, Prince Alfred, Prince Octavius, Princess Elizabeth, Princess Mary, Princess Sophia and Princess Amelia were all born between 1765 and 1783. The death of two of the King's brothers removed a potential source of trouble. George's youngest brother Frederick died on 29 December 1765, aged fifteen, and Edward Augustus, Duke of York, died on 17 September 1767, aged twenty-eight. The Duke of York had been something of an embarrassment. He was less serious and less obedient than the King and had always been his sisters' favourite. Moreover, he had never been dominated by his mother. He seemed to be a very promising naval officer and was a great

60

Tapestry portraits of the younger children of George III. Left to right, top row: Princess Elizabeth; Ernest, Duke of Cumberland; Augustus, Duke of Sussex; Adolphus, Duke of Cambridge; Bottom row: Princess Mary; Princess Sophia; Prince Octavius and Prince Alfred.

Prince Ernest Augustus

Prince Augustus Frederic

Prince Adolphus Frederic

Princess Sophia

Prince Octavius

Prince Alfred

success with women. At the age of eighteen, unmoved by
Augusta's pleas not to make himself common and secretly
encouraged by George II, he began an affair with the Countess
of Essex. This lady was followed by the Duchess of Richmond –
sister-in-law of Lady Sarah Lennox – Lady Mary Coke and
Lady Anne Stanhope, to name but a few. Lady Mary Coke, in
particular, was most offensive to the Queen. George, upright
and respectable, strongly disapproved of Edward's behaviour.
Underneath the King's pious exterior there was probably a hint
of jealousy of his uninhibited brother.

61

Pitt's government was something of a hotch-potch, Edmund Burke described it as 'a mosaic administration' but its formation made the Crown more popular than at any time since George's accession. The City of London prepared for a massive firework display. Suddenly it was announced that Pitt had accepted a peerage and become Earl of Chatham. The celebrations were cancelled and the popular hero was denounced as courtier and royal dupe. His desertion of the people was compared to Strafford's in 1628. Pitt was a great war leader, but lacked the quality of a peace-time Premier. His Ministers were talented, but their diverse opinions demanded great tact, and there was a haughtiness about Pitt which was bound to provoke resentment.

The harvest of 1766 failed and one of Chatham's first actions was to issue an Order in Council prohibiting the export of corn. Opposition members questioned the legality of the proclamation but George vigorously supported his Ministers. The King worked harder and harder; in September 1766 he was checking precedents for Pitt's proclamation, making detailed arrangements for the marriage of his sister Caroline to King Christian VII of Denmark, examining prisoners convicted for taking part in the recent riots and inquiring into the state of the East India Company. In the summer of 1766 George and Charlotte began

to appear more in society and visited several great houses, including Horace Walpole's strange 'Gothick' mansion at Strawberry Hill.

Chatham's conduct provoked the resignation of several Ministers; the aristocracy hated him, the people thought he had betrayed them and the King seemed his only friend. The Prime Minister became ill, retired to Bath and left his colleagues to struggle on as best they could. On several occasions the government was defeated in Parliament but, such was George's dread of Grenville, that he would not listen to talk of resignation. Chatham's health was vital; George sent letters, offered to visit his minister's sick-bed and was reduced to begging for even a quarter of an hour's conversation and advice. Unfortunately Chatham was suffering from a nervous break-down which made him incapable of any effort.

For a time it seemed that Charles Townshend, the Chancellor of the Exchequer, would hold the ministry together. Townshend appeared to have a brilliant future and was at his best when delivering what were politely described as 'Champagne Speeches'. He was always reckless and, wishing to conciliate Grenville, produced another scheme for taxing the American colonies. In Chatham's absence, his colleagues were browbeaten into accepting these proposals which Townshend introduced on 13 May 1767. The plan to tax glass, paper, paint and tea imported into America from Britain was an ingenious one. Townshend argued that the articles taxed were not the product of American labour and the duties were simply a small payment to Britain towards the heavy cost of maintaining the freedom of the seas. The Americans benefited almost as much from the protection of the Royal Navy as the King's British subjects. The Bill was passed with hardly any opposition. Chatham's illness became worse and he could take no part in public affairs for the next eighteen months. Townshend died suddenly on 4 September 1767 at the age of forty-two, and the Duke of Grafton became effective Prime Minister.

Early in 1768 John Wilkes returned to England. Although a convicted outlaw, Wilkes believed that fear of popular disturbance would prevent the government taking any action against him. He could scarcely have chosen a better time; high food prices were angering the poorer areas of London and a

RIGHT John Stuart, 3rd
Earl of Bute; painted by
Joshua Reynolds in 1773.
BELOW Princess Augusta
of Saxe–Gotha, mother of
George III. This portrait
was painted in about 1736
by Charles Philips.

general election was at hand. Wilkes decided to stand for Middlesex and it was soon evident that he had lost none of his popularity with the masses. In Piccadilly private carriages were stopped and 'No. 45' scratched on the panels. The King had no time for rioters and violence stirred up by outlaws. George's name was insulted and an attack expected on Buckingham House. The King declared 'I only wish the rioters would make the attempt in order that I might have an opportunity of dispersing them at the head of my Guards.'

Wilkes was elected, but the King demanded his arrest and expulsion from Parliament; he wanted vengeance on Wilkes for stirring up the people, for advocating atheism and for his crude abuse of the Dowager Princess of Wales. It was too late; either Wilkes should have been pardoned and everyone would have soon forgotten him, or he should have been arrested before he could begin his campaign. George never appreciated the dangers of making martyrs; he was like Grenville in believing that the law must take its course regardless of the consequences. London was in great excitement and the King convinced that property must be protected even if troops had to fire on the crowds. George's attitude may have been insensitive, but at least it was preferable to Grafton's; the acting Prime Minister simply panicked and left London for 'rural retirement and the arms of a faded beauty'.

Several London trades, including the watermen, came out on strike. The gates at Richmond Lodge were shut and the strikers were not allowed to see the King. Parliament assembled on 9 May 1768 but Wilkes did not appear and so the mob went to the King's Bench Prison to release him. Soldiers had to be called in, six people were killed and fifteen wounded. The King wrote to Viscount Weymouth 'bloodshed is not what I delight in but it seems to me the only way of restoring a due obedience to the laws'. George was not the man to inquire whether those laws were really to the advantage of all his subjects. Fortunately the London mob was not united against the King and on 14 May the watermen attacked Wilkes's supporters.

Wilkes was brought before the House of Commons and expelled for the second time on 3 February 1769. King and Ministers were furious when the Middlesex electors insisted on re-electing Wilkes. A number of leading City merchants tried

'Bloodshed is not what I delight in but it seems to me the only way of restoring a due obedience to the laws'

66

to take an address to St James's Palace expressing their loyalty to the throne and their detestation of Wilkes. The hostility of crowds in the streets forced many to abandon their journey. Just before the rioting reached St James's a hearse drew up at the main entrance of the Palace. On the sides of the vehicle were pictures of the recent shootings and on the roof stood a man dressed as an executioner. At such moments, the fate of Charles I cannot have been far from George's mind. The King behaved with dignity and Lord Holland reported that he gave no indication either in appearance or in conversation that anything was unusual.

It was not only Wilkes who disturbed the routine of Court life. In August 1768 the nineteen-year-old King of Denmark and his Queen, George's sister Caroline, visited England. The marriage had not been a success and Christian's wild life distressed his brother-in-law. The King of England had experienced the temptations of youth, but he had overcome them; although Christian was young, George expected him to behave properly. The King attempted to conceal his distaste. Gold plate was brought specially from the Tower in honour of the guests, but there were lapses in the hospitality and the King of Denmark was forced to arrive at St James's Palace in a hired carriage. George had reason for jealousy. Every foreign monarch visiting England seemed to be more popular with the people than their own King. Christian was showered with honorary degrees, banquets and celebrations, but the diminutive King of Denmark, a boy with wide-ranging sexual tastes, did not care for formality all the time. He dressed himself as an ordinary sailor and spent his nights in the taverns and brothels of St Giles, Holborn. To George's horror, knowledge of these activities only increased Christian's popularity. The King might have realised that his own image was far too much that of a prig, and that his people always liked a King who showed himself human. Among the London masses there was a strong feeling that a monarch was never more properly engaged than in debauchery.

During Chatham's illness, his colleagues did not cover themselves with glory. In addition to their other follies they allowed France to seize Corsica; if the Duke of Grafton had been more resolute, Napoleon Bonaparte might have been a British subject. Chatham had been almost forgotten, but in October 1768

he began to recover. He was horrified when told what had happened and insisted on resigning. The Duke of Grafton – like Richmond, a descendant of Charles II – now became Prime Minister in name as well as in practice. Despite Grafton's wealth and territorial influence, he was not a good choice. If Grenville worked too hard, Grafton was too idle and spent most of his time at race meetings. According to Horace Walpole, he only deigned to come to London once a fortnight. When he did so, he outraged polite society by flaunting his mistress, the notorious Nancy Parsons, and on one occasion took her to a gala performance at Covent Garden when the Queen was present. The eighteenth-century Court smiled on discreet dalliance, but it insisted on outward propriety almost as much as in Victorian days. In any case his own behaviour meant that he lost the opportunity to make any political capital out of Wilkes's immorality.

Chatham's recovery continued and his appearance at a levée in July 1769 scared Grafton and his friends half out of their wits. When Parliament assembled on 9 January 1770 Chatham was in his old form and attacked Grafton on topics ranging from Corsica to the treatment of Wilkes. The Lord Chancellor, Lord Cambden, declared that the speech had opened his eyes; he then proceeded to denounce his own colleagues whose violence and tyranny had alienated the people from the King, unless things were changed, those who had the welfare of the constitution at heart would take matters into their own hands. The Ministers were under attack from all sides. Lord Rockingham had drawn many lessons from his own dismissal. On 22 January he came close to denouncing the King himself. He declared that discontent had increased and the real standing of the Crown diminished ever since George came to the throne. There had been a deliberate campaign to extend the King's prerogative and destroy the liberties of the subject. Unless George acted quickly, a hostile opposition would force itself into office entirely against the King's wishes. Instead of facing his enemies, Grafton resigned and left George at the mercy of his foes, with no friend to turn to.

AFTER SOME HESITATION, George asked Grafton's Chancellor of the Exchequer, Lord Frederick North, the member for Banbury, to form a government. North has gone down in history as the worst Prime Minister of all time, 'the man who lost America'. Although few premiers have been more unfortunate than North, there have been many who have been far less able. In fact, North was much more satisfactory than Grafton to the King. His private life was virtuous, he was unconnected with the over-mighty Whig families, he was unlikely to repeat Grenville's insolence and he had no time for Wilkes and rabble-rousing. It was several years before George came to regret his choice.

The new Prime Minister was not prepossessing in appearance. His eyes rolled about, his face seemed blown up and, combined with his thick lips, he must have had something of the air of a blind trumpeter. But no Prime Minister could remain in office as long as North without possessing great ability; in fact, after Townshend's death, he was probably the best debater in the House of Commons. His grasp of finance, knowledge of precedents and feeling for the mood of the House were unrivalled. Unlike the ill-tempered Grenville, he was good-humoured and generally 'unflappable'. On one occasion an opposition member, imagining North to be asleep on the Treasury bench, thundered 'even now the noble Lord is slumbering over the ruin of his country'; as he opened his eyes, North interjected 'I wish to Heaven that I was'. The new Prime Minister always seemed able to make his enemies' arguments ridiculous and even his great adversary, Charles Fox, admitted that he knew no one who could speak with such mastery of language on any subject. He was always plausible and always concise. He would have been a great success in peace time.

All the denunciations intended for Grafton were turned on North but, unlike much greater men, the Prime Minister was never disturbed by what people said about him. Far from being a would-be despot, he was first and last a Parliament man, the King's friend but a professional politician to the finger tips. Whatever his difficulties, he always looked forward to a new session of Parliament with pleasure.

There was an unpleasant dispute between Parliament and the City which Wilkes attempted to exploit. The Speaker's mess-

enger was imprisoned in the Mansion House, and Parliament retaliated by sending the Lord Mayor to the Tower. The people supported the Mayor and aldermen; North was jostled and the King hit by an apple on his way to Westminster. Thereafter, North had the sense to stop persecuting Wilkes, who soon sank into the relative obscurity of a City magistrate, disavowed his old politics and actually attended levées. One day the King asked Wilkes about his 'old friend' Sergeant Glyn who had represented him at his trial. Wilkes was indignant: 'My *friend* Sire; he is no friend of mine; he was a Wilkite which I never was.'

After the initial difficulties, politics settled down and became more stable than at any time since George's accession. So complete was North's ascendancy that very little of note happened at Westminster between 1771 and 1774. The King could appear less directly involved and his popularity gradually increased. The country was prosperous again and many causes of friction had disappeared. George Grenville, Alderman Beckford and the Princess Dowager were dead and Wilkes was silent. By the time the King reached his early thirties, he was no longer a green boy but a successful politician in his own right who would never again submit to being pushed around by those who were supposed to be his servants.

Political tranquility gave the King more time for domestic life. As a boy, he often showed an elder brother's hauteur at the follies of those who were only a few years his junior. In later life he had much to complain of. His brothers the Duke of Cumberland and the Duke of Gloucester both married unsuitable widows. The Duchess of Cumberland was described as having 'the most amorous eyes in the world and eyelashes a yard long; coquette beyond measure, artful as Cleopatra and completely mistress of her passions'. The Duchess of Gloucester was the illegitimate daughter of a milliner who had already done well by marrying the aged Earl Waldegrave. The Duke of Gloucester married in 1766 but George did not find out until 1774, and then refused to make any provision for his brother's family. Unlike the rest of his family, who preferred the Duke of York, Gloucester was George's favourite brother and the King was very hurt by what he regarded as an act of betrayal to the

74

The RECEPTION in 1760.

The Reception in 1770 in our next.

The RECEPTION in 1770.

honour of the House of Hanover. In later years, the King wished for a reconciliation but still believed that he would scandalise all the crowned heads of Europe by inviting the Duchess to Court.

The greatest family disaster was the fate of the Queen of Denmark. George's sister was only fifteen at the time of her marriage to Christian VII, and Sir Joshua Reynolds claimed that he could not do justice to the bride because she was constantly in tears when he was trying to paint her. After returning from his visit to England, Christian seems to have infected his wife with venereal disease. The formerly quiet and withdrawn Queen became noisy and eccentric; she dressed almost continually in a man's black riding habit with a large black slouch hat. She consulted a German doctor, John Struensee, who managed to cure, or at least to arrest, her disease. Caroline was neglected by her husband and disgusted by his taste for prostitutes and boys. It was not long before she became Struensee's mistress and made little secret of their relationship. Soon prints were on sale all over Copenhagen showing the couple together. At first, Christian appeared to connive at his wife's adultery, but on the night of 17 January 1772, Caroline and Struensee were arrested and the Queen taken under armed guard to the fortress of Kronberg where she heard that her lover had been executed with the most extreme barbarity.

There was a possibility that Caroline too would be executed, but Denmark was a weak country and England an extremely powerful one. As soon as he heard of his sister's imprisonment, George drew up plans to send a naval force to the Baltic to persuade the Danes to release his sister. It was one of the first examples of 'Gun Boat Diplomacy'. Although George felt sorry for Caroline, she was a disgraced and dishonoured woman who could not return to the English Court. She retired to the Castle of Zell in Hanover and died there on 10 May 1775, aged twenty-three.

These were heavy blows but George was strong enough to take them. Away from St James's, domestic life was pleasantly informal. In the summer of 1775 George and Charlotte stayed at the White House, since demolished, in what is now Kew Gardens. King and Queen got up at six and spent two hours alone before breakfasting with their elder children. George believed in exercise, plenty of air and a simple, almost vegetarian

OPPOSITE Portrait of George III painted at the studio of Allan Ramsay in 1767.

diet. At Kew he went for long walks, occasionally played on a harpsichord once owned by Handel, enjoyed a game of backgammon with his equerries, or prayed alone in a small chapel with a prayer book in which all references to 'our most religious and gracious King' were struck out and replaced with the words 'a most miserable sinner'.

George never conformed to the picture of the hard-drinking, over-eating, corpulent Englishman supposedly typical of the time. He had a very modern horror of overweight; obesity ran in his family and as a young man he resolved never to become the size of his huge uncles. In fact the King preserved a youthful figure well into middle age. Between breakfast and dinner he usually ate only one slice of bread and butter and a 'dish' of black tea. After his illness in 1765, George enjoyed excellent health for over twenty years. Even in bad weather, he thought nothing of riding from Windsor to London, holding a levée and a meeting of the Privy Council and then riding back to Windsor.

No one could accuse George of cowardice. He kept calm in the face of anarchy throughout London when his Ministers trembled; in 1779, and even in 1805, he was ready to take command of his armies in the event of invasion. But it was not all Germanic duty and seriousness. He was relaxed in the company of his children and – once the initial reserve had been overcome – he showed the same qualities to his Ministers. He loved to tease Lord Chancellor Eldon and the Archbishop of Canterbury, Dr Manners Sutton, that both had eloped with their wives. George took an interest in music and the theatre – his taste was not over-refined and his main love was for rather obvious farce, although Mrs Siddons and David Garrick were called to Buckingham House to read to the King and Queen.

Whether serious or in jest, in his family life or in the affairs of State, one of the most fundamental aspects of George's character was his strong religious faith. It was a narrow creed and has been blamed for giving him all sorts of repressions and complexes. It is taking things too far to try to find in this a psychological explanation for George's subsequent illness. In fact, religion was almost certainly a stabilising influence which helped the King face difficult situations calmly, while men who were his intellectual superiors completely lost their heads. It was a childlike

George III's youngest sister, Caroline Matilda, had been married to Christian VII of Denmark in 1766. The marriage was a disaster, for the Danish King was a vicious profligate, and Caroline turned for consolation to a German doctor, John Struensee.
ABOVE LEFT Engraving showing the arrest of Caroline for adultery in January 1772. She was taken to the fortress of Kronberg, while her lover was cruelly put to death.

ABOVE RIGHT Satire
portraying Bute at work
on his plans to establish
absolute power, but
troubled by a
visitation from the ghost
of Struensee.

and intensely personal faith in which verses from the Psalms
seemed to go to the heart of George's own problems. One
morning, towards the end of his reign, when the King was very
worried by the political situation, he visibly started at a verse
from the *Venite* and repeated it to himself several times during
the service: 'Forty years long was I grieved with this generation
and said: it is a people that do err in their hearts for they have not
known my ways.' George was a staunch Protestant and had a
real horror of Roman Catholicism. If he wished for any change
in the Church of England it was that it should remove all
remaining traces of Catholicism. As a Protestant and 'rational
man' the King disapproved of the Athanasian Creed with its
frequent use of the word 'Catholic' and its assertion of the ultimate incomprehensibility of the Godhead. George refused to
say this creed himself and discreetly supported an unsuccessful
campaign for its removal from the prayer book. He was something of a Puritan and was horrified to learn that a ball had been
held at Lambeth Palace. He wrote to Dr Cornwallis: 'these
levities and vain dissipations are utterly inexpedient, if not un-
lawful, to pass in a residence for many centuries devoted to
divine studies, religious retirement and the extensive exercise of
charity and benevolence'. To non-conformists, especially

Methodists, he was well-disposed and gave generously to a fund for building a German Protestant Church in London.

Through religion, the King became interested in education, and looked forward to the day when every poor child in the country would be able to read his Bible. At a time when many regarded popular education as dangerous, George gave it his steady support. Even if he was not really interested, he was able to talk to his subjects about advances in science, the condition of the Presbyterian clergy, poetry, book-collecting, astronomy – everything under the sun, with at least a smattering of knowledge. In short, in day-to-day life, George III was a splendid King who behaved much better than his brother monarchs. Sir Robert Murray, who was presented to Louis XVI at Fontainebleau in November 1774, declared: 'The King receives presentations with less attention than one naturally shows to a cat. I doubt if there is a King of Nègres or a Khan of Tartare so ridiculously uncivil. For us, who know our own King, who would speak civilly to even a French Captain, how strange must this appear.' Even those who disliked George's policies admitted his good points. Benjamin Franklin, who visited London during the riots of May 1768, commented: 'Some punishment seems preparing for a People who are so ungratefully abusing the best Constitution and the best King any nation was ever blessed with.' Punishment was coming, but George was to suffer from it as much as any of his ungrateful people.

The first half of the 1770s may have been quiet in England, but in America there were increasing signs of trouble. The King was still popular, and as late as 1768 the Assembly of Virginia voted money for a statue of George III. The atmosphere was more hostile in Massachusetts; Henry Otis began to criticise not just one set of Ministers but the attitudes and failings of all leading English politicians:

> They have no education but travelling through France from whence they return full of the slavish principles of that country. They know nothing of business when they come into their offices and do not stay long in them to acquire that little knowledge which is gained by experience.

Ministers constantly misrepresented American opinion in their

OPPOSITE The three younger daughters of George III, the Princesses Mary, Sophia and Amelia. Painting by J. Singleton Copley.

81

reports to the King. According to Lord Hillsborough, discontent was merely the work of insolent rabble-rousing demagogues. George's prejudices were strengthened by public opinion in Britain. The country gentlemen supported the government because they hoped that the new source of revenue from the colonies would mean that the land tax could be reduced. When Parliament met in November 1768, votes of censure were passed on the Massachusetts Assembly and addresses presented to the King assuring him of popular support for any measures necessary to maintain his authority in America.

As Grafton's Chancellor of the Exchequer, Lord North had been in favour of a tough line with the colonists. On the taxation issue he declared 'I will never yield till I have seen America at my feet.' North did agree, however, to the repeal of all Townshend's duties, except that on tea. Tea was becoming very popular in England but it was still something of a rarity in America. The consumption was so low that the Treasury would derive about £3000 a year from the duty. No one could claim that the Americans were heavily taxed. The issue of principle was still bitterly contested, but North's measure was enough to end the boycott of British goods in all colonies except Massachusetts. In the early 1770s George received a number of petitions from the Colonies protesting against the tax and against the behaviour of many of his representatives in North America. Even if he had favoured the petitions, George had no choice but to submit them to the Privy Council and accept the opinion of that body. A petition against the Governor of Massachusetts was heard at the Cockpit in Whitehall on 29 January 1774. The petitioners were represented by Benjamin Franklin, the agent of the American Colonies in Britain. Franklin, who had hitherto been pro-British, was viciously attacked and humiliated by the Solicitor-General, Alexander Wedderburn. The Council advised the King that the petition was 'groundless, vexatious and scandalous' and recommended Franklin's dismissal as Deputy Paymaster-General for America.

The Americans did more than petition. In December 1773 a tea-ship belonging to the East India Company was attacked in Boston harbour by a large number of citizens, some so unwilling to compromise their official positions that they disguised themselves as Mohawk Indians. At 'The Boston Tea Party' a cargo

OPPOSITE Education in eighteenth-century England.
ABOVE The trade card for a private French Boarding School in Chelsea. This kind of school offered the type of education acceptable to young ladies of respectability.
BELOW 'The Hopes of the Family' – one of a series of scenes of University life engraved by Bunbury of Clare College, Cambridge, and published in 1774.

82

SLOANE HOUSE.

Terms of Mrs Chassaings

FRENCH BOARDING SCHOOL,

Sloane Street, CHELSEA.

Board and Education

including FRENCH *grammatically by* Mr *Chassaing,*

At 30 Guineas per Annum,

Day Boarders 15 Guineas per Annum.

Music, Dancing, Drawing, Writing & Accounts,

Geography with the use of the Globes at

One Guinea p^r Qua^{ter} & a Guinea entrance each

Italian 2 Guineas p^r Quarter and One

Guinea entrance.

Every Lady has a separate Bed.

1797

George III and Astronomy

The King was particularly interested in astronomy and was a generous patron to the Royal Society. In 1781 William Herschel discovered the planet Uranus, and was persuaded by George III to give up his career as a musician and to become his private astronomer. Herschel made many important astronomical discoveries and became the first president of the Royal Astronomical Society.

RIGHT The King's celestial globe.
OPPOSITE An engraving of William Herschel's telescope made in 1775. The telescope was constructed under the patronage of George III.
BELOW The loadstone and case belonging to George III and stamped with his arms.

Fig. 1.

worth £18,000 was destroyed. Although the Americans were
being taxed without their consent, the duty on tea was only
threepence per pound – a quarter of the tax paid by English
tea-drinkers.

Opinion in Britain was outraged by the events in Boston. As
a reprisal, North suspended the Massachusetts Charter, ordered
the closure of Boston harbour and the transfer of its trade to
Salem, abolished the elected Council of Massachusetts for one
nominated by the Crown and allowed the Governor to choose
all judges and magistrates. North's proposals were carried by
large majorities in Parliament but they brought the other
American colonies, hitherto lukewarm in opposition, onto the
side of the people of Boston. In September 1775 a General Continental Congress met in Philadelphia, more British troops
were sent to America and the colonies began training their
militia forces. A clash between redcoats and 'minutemen' was
inevitable and the escalation of events from a minor skirmish at
Concord and then on to Bunker's Hill, early British victories,
American recovery culminating in the surrender of General
Burgoyne at Saratoga might have been foreseen. Although the
British might win victories, the continent was too vast for
European armies to hold down in defiance of the colonists. A
political solution was the only answer.

George was aware of the dangers of the American situation,
although he did not appreciate their full magnitude. The King
had no desire to impose a 'tyranny' on his American subjects nor
did he in any sense 'plan' the war against them. If possible he

wanted to avoid hostilities but his ideas of compromise were usually too little too late. George made contact with Franklin through their mutual friend Lord Howe but nothing came of his private initiative. The British ruling classes believed that because the Americans had no aristocracy with a military tradition, they were bound to be cowards and thus capable of being subdued. The King had broadened his social contacts since his days at Leicester House but, although he loved his people, he had little contact with those who did not belong to the landed classes. George refused to let himself be dominated by an aristocratic clique but he had a high appreciation of the virtues of aristocracy – loyalty to the Crown, military prowess, territorial influence, the respect of other sections of society and leadership in all the arts of civilisation. If the House of Lords and their relations in the Commons gave North large majorities then the Prime Minister must be right. That was the order of nature. Benjamin Franklin's rejection of the caste superiority claimed by Parliament and an indirect assertion of the need for a reform of the representative system would have filled George with horror.

So long as the war was going reasonably well, there were few in any section of society who gave much thought to the abstract justice of the American cause. Pleas for conciliation from Chatham and Rockingham fell on deaf ears. The King was far more in tune with the mood of the nation when he described the Americans as an 'unhappy, misled, deluded multitude'. Attempts were still made at compromise, but the demand in America for complete separation from Britain was increasing. For some time there was great reluctance to blame George, and the British forces were described as the Parliamentary, not the Royal armies. Only after the Declaration of Independence – issued by Congress on 4 July 1776 – was it necessary to depict the King as a tyrant. Recent statues and pictures were smashed to pieces.

The British troops fought extremely well and were generally supported by the Indian population who feared that with independence their territories would be taken away far more ruthlessly than under the British. Despite Indian support, however, the British Commanders seemed unable to follow up their victories. Lord North began to doubt their competence:

'I do not know whether our Generals will frighten the enemy but I know they frighten me whenever I think of them.' The news of the failure of an attempt to invade New York from Canada and Burgoyne's surrender came as a tremendous blow. George was very upset but, according to Horace Walpole, tried to disguise his concern by laughing and being so indecently merry that Lord North had to stop him. The disaster had an important effect on politics. The country gentlemen began to complain that the war was very expensive without producing any tangible results. Even worse, Saratoga gave France an excuse to recognise the colonies as an independent state, receive Franklin at Versailles and negotiate an alliance with him. The war in America was a splendid opportunity for France to smash the maritime and colonial superiority which Britain had established in the Seven Years War. Much of the British navy was engaged in operations off the east coast of America; the Channel was very vulnerable. The King sent James Hutton to Paris in a last attempt to get terms from Franklin. It was clear that there would be increasing pressure to give the Americans peace at any price in order to concentrate on an enemy nearer at home.

After seven years as Premier, North had become weary. He wanted to obtain peace with the rebels and then retire. In February 1778 he offered the Americans any terms short of actual independence. But independence had become a fact and the suggestion was poorly received. George would not allow the Prime Minister to retire and begged North not to follow Grafton's example by deserting him in his hour of need.

As war with France drew near there were demands that Chatham should become Prime Minister. North himself urged the King to send for a man who was probably the greatest war leader in British history. George would not hear of the suggestion. Despite his sense of national duty, he would not give office to a man he considered had betrayed him. The King had been kind and tolerant when Chatham was ill and the Earl owed his peerage and a pension of £5,000 per year to George's favour. Chatham's inflammatory speeches attacking North and vindicating his rebels had made him 'the trumpet of sedition', ready to go to the edge of treason to destroy his political enemies. George would probably have been forced to come to terms with Chatham, but the great statesman had a stroke in the

The able Doctor, or America Swallowing the Bitter Draught.

House of Lords and died on 11 May 1778. The King was displeased when Parliament voted that Chatham, the last remaining great figure from George II's reign, should have a public funeral in Westminster Abbey.

The set-backs to North's American policy gave new hope to the opposition, particularly to the Whig grandees. The Earl of Chatham had been too much of an individualist to be completely acceptable either to the Crown or to the great families. After Chatham's death, the spiritual heirs of the Duke of Newcastle sought to regain their hegemony. George was a healthy man of forty and there was no prospect of another reign in the forseeable future. There was no point in opposition members pinning their hopes on sympathetic members of the Royal Family. The only way they could obtain the offices which they regarded as theirs by right was to oppose the King and Lord North on points of principle, defeat the government in Parliament and compel George to give them what they wanted.

The Whig grandees were prepared to go to extreme lengths and use popular discontent – which could very easily recoil – to achieve their aims. As they no longer enjoyed lucrative sinecure

Cartoon showing an American being forcibly made to drink tea, following the retention of Townshend's duty on the beverage.

89

Bunkers hill or the blessed effects of Family quarrels

17 June 1775

places, they began to argue that these appointments were evil and the means by which the King exercised undesirable influence over Parliament. On 8 February 1780 Sir George Saville presented 'The Yorkshire Petition' urging the abolition of sinecures. War with the American colonies disrupted trade, and merchants claimed that they had difficulty in finding the money to pay their taxes. Some of the proceeds of this taxation went into the pockets of men who gave the country nothing in return. The time had come for drastic reductions.

The Whigs secured the services of the great Irish orator Edmund Burke. On 11 February 1780 Burke introduced his 'Plan of Economical Reform' in which he attacked the influence of the Crown as having taken away vigour from arms, wisdom from government and every shadow of credit from kingship. Although Burke's plan was defeated, later that year John Dunning's motion 'that the influence of the Crown has increased, is increasing and ought to be diminished' was carried by a majority of eighteen. It was a clear sign that the tide was turning against North.

In many ways the strategy employed by Rockingham and his followers was masterly. The country gentlemen and merchants had a real interest in abolishing sinecures and reducing taxation. For the Whig grandees, however, what began simply as a device to obtain office could become something which was extremely difficult to control. The aristocrats of France took a very similar path a few years later. Some of the Whigs were so carried away by the oratory of Burke and Charles Fox that they really came to believe that George wanted to be an absolute monarch. Others realised that promises made in opposition might be embarrassing when they gained office; some of their new allies might force them to honour obligations they never intended to keep. It was all very well to reduce the King's influence, but the next step would be to examine the unconstitutional influence of aristocrats controlling as many as a dozen seats in the House of Commons. If such questions were raised, the Marquess of Rockingham, for one, would feel very uncomfortable indeed. There was both cynicism and idealism among the Whigs – probably more of the first than the second. The King saw this and hoped that it would not be long before his accusers realised the inevitable consequences of their actions.

Pub. by E. Dachery Aprill 24 1783 St James Street

G EORGE WAS UPSET by the bitter and unfair speeches, but he did not let them disturb his quiet domestic life. He lived at Kew from May to November and only went to London on Wednesdays and Fridays. On 28 June 1779, the Prince of Wales's birthday, the Royal Family visited Bulstrode Park in Buckinghamshire and saw Mrs Delany, an old lady who had been a friend of Swift.

The King drove the Queen in an open chaise. The Prince of Wales and Prince Frederick rode on horseback; all with proper attendants but no guards. Princess Royal and Lady Weymouth in a post chaise; Princess Augusta, Princess Elizabeth, Prince Adolphus, about seven years old, and Lady Charlotte Finch [governess to the younger children] in a coach; another coach full of attendant gentlemen. These with all their attendants in rank and file, made a splendid figure as they drove through the park and round up to the House. The Queen was in a hat, and an Italian night [i.e. evening] -gown of purple Lute string, trimmed with silver gauze. She is graceful and genteel; the King's condescension and good humour took off all awe but what one must have for so respectable a character, severely tried by his enemies at home, as well as abroad. The King and all the men were in uniform, blue and gold. They walked through the great apartments, which are in a line, and attentively observed everything, the pictures in particular. The King desired me to show the Queen one of my books of plants. She seated herself in the gallery; a table and a book laid before her. I kept my distance till she called me to ask some questions about the mosaic paper work, and as I stood before her majesty, the King set a chair behind me. I turned with some hesitation and confusion, on receiving so great an honour, when the Queen said 'Mrs Delany, sit down, sit down: it is not everybody that has a chair brought her by a King.'

Later Mrs Delany was entertained at Windsor Castle:

At eight the King came into the room with so much cheerfulness and good humour, that it is impossible to feel any painful restriction. It was the hour of the King and the Queen, and eleven of the Princes and Princesses walking on the terrace. We sat in the bay window, well pleased with our companions and the brilliant show on the terrace, on which we looked; the band of music playing all the time under the window. When they returned, we were summoned into the next room for tea, and the royals began a ball and danced two country-dances to the music of French horns, bassoons

ABOVE Mrs Delany, painted by Opie in 1782. RIGHT Queen Charlotte in 1780. Windsor Castle is depicted in the background with a family group of thirteen of the royal children. Portrait by Benjamin West.

PREVIOUS PAGES The levée at St James's Palace in 1783, showing Lord North and Fox holding the King's head on a pole.

94

The Royal Academy

In 1768, a Royal Academy of Arts in London was set up under the patronage of George III, 'for the purpose of cultivating and improving the arts of painting, sculpture and architecture'. The first president, Sir Joshua Reynolds, held the post until his death in 1792. There was considerable feeling amongst the artistic circles concerning the success of Reynolds and the limitations imposed upon painting by the establishment of an academy run on rigid principles. Artists such as William Blake remained outside the establishment, and thus were not looked upon with favour by the King.

ABOVE A meeting of the Royal Academy, with Sir Joshua Reynolds seated just left of centre.
LEFT Illustration from William Blake's *Urizen*, showing figures from his complex mythology, Los, Enitharmon and Orc.

BELOW Painting by George Stubbs of two Indians with the cheetah which was presented to George III.

and hautboys, which were the same that played on the terrace. The King came up to the Prince of Wales and said how great an effort it must be to play that kind of music so long a time together.

Mrs Delany was no stranger to royalty; as a girl she had been a maid-of-honour to Queen Anne. Even so, there is a tremendous deference about her accounts, a sheer amazement that the King behaved like an ordinary gentleman. Mrs Delany may have been old-fashioned, but her outlook was probably that of most of the King's subjects. Some of the mystique of the Crown may have been eroded, but George's image was closer to the demi-god sovereign of Tudor times than to twentieth-century notions of monarchy. There were still people who believed the King possessed magical powers and that his Touch would cure scrofula. The country gentry and the middle classes – lawyers and professional men as well as merchants – might be willing to help the Whigs reduce George's powers, but if they felt that the politicians had overstepped the mark, their sympathies would return to the King. It was a consideration that the Whigs would forget at their peril.

George was strong in moral courage. It took him a long time to make up his mind, but having done so, he was immovable. He was not the most intelligent of monarchs; when it was a question of suitable persons to be made judges or bishops, the King was in his element but, despite all his efforts, he could never grasp complicated questions of finance or the principles of colonial and legal reform. In some ways he was over-rigid – too concerned about external respectability and absolutely fanatical about punctuality. Critics called his firmness ignorance, prejudice and obstinacy. But these very defects gave him a sense of honour and truthfulness and a determination to stand by those who stood by him. Such qualities are not always wise in a king but they do suggest that George was a better man than many of his predecessors.

The King's authority and courage was strikingly demon-strated in the terrible days of the Gordon Riots in June 1780. Lord George Gordon, a nephew of the Duke of Atholl and godson of George II, was a Protestant fanatic, determined to use any means to reverse minor concessions given to Roman Catholics in 1778. For a week, 'The Protestant Association' – in reality a mob driven berserk by hysterical oratory and an unlimited supply of gin – had London at its feet. In Parliament, Gordon told the Prime Minister that at a word from him the mob would tear members of the Cabinet to pieces. Roman Catholic chapels and business premises were attacked and burned; soon London was facing its worst fire since 1666.

The magistrates seemed powerless and the Lord Chancellor sat trembling like a leaf in the House of Lords, but the King's mind was made up. He called a meeting of the Privy Council and, with the assistance of the Attorney General, obtained a ruling that soldiers were justified in firing upon rioters and looters without the formality of first reading the Riot Act. George was prepared to lead his Guards in dispersing the rabble. He added 'I lament the conduct of the magistrates, but I can answer for *one* [pointing to himself] *one* who will do his duty'. Before order was restored, over three hundred people had been killed; in one incident, rioters in Fleet Street launched a frontal attack on the military. George's solution may seem brutal but it was the only way to restore sanity to a capital which had gone mad. If the authorities had not been shaken out of their indecision, the destruction and loss of life would have been much greater.

'*I can answer for one … who will do his duty*'

Despite his majesty and authority, the King experienced the same joys and sorrows as other men. He wept when his son the Duke of York left England for a military academy in Prussia; unfortunately there were more permanent separations. The offspring of kings and aristocrats had a better chance of survival than those of the poor, but almost every family in the land would lose some of their children in infancy. At a time when doctors often did more harm than good, the odds were not entirely in favour of the rich. The King and Queen were more fortunate than most parents. Their youngest son Alfred died, aged two, on 20 August 1782. As the boy was dying, George read aloud a sermon by Dr Blair which ended with a description of the Church Triumphant from the Book of Revelations. While the King was reading, a knock was heard at the door, he shuddered but went on. When he had finished, he went to Charlotte and said 'Such, my dearest, I humbly trust our little Alfred now is. That knock informed me he is passed from death into life.' But Alfred was not George's favourite son; he told the Queen 'I am very sorry for Alfred but had it been Octavius, I should have

An Exact Representation of the Burning, Plunderin
on the memorable 7th of

London Published as the Act directs, July 10th 1781, by P. Mitchell North Audley Street Grosvenor S.

truction of NEWGATE *by the Rioters,*

H. Roberts sc.

N.º 23. Pater Noster Row.

In June 1780 the Gordon Riots broke out in London. The mob was led by Lord George Gordon, a Protestant fanatic marching under the 'No Popery' banner. On 7 June, Newgate was attacked and fired, despite attempts by the military to restore order.

William Pitt the Younger;
bust made by J. Nollekens
in 1808, two years after
Pitt's death.

died too.' Nine months later, Octavius did die – a few weeks
after his fourth birthday. The King was terribly distressed, but
had sufficient strength of character to bear his burden. On 7
August 1783, the Queen gave birth to her fifteenth and last
child, Princess Amelia, who succeeded Octavius in her father's
affections.

Apart from the Gordon Riots, 1780 gave some respite after
recent disasters. Admiral Rodney achieved a great victory
against the Spanish fleet in the West Indies and was able to raise
the siege of Gibraltar. When the Dutch joined the war against

England, Rodney repeated his triumphs. These successes meant that the newly-elected House of Commons which met on 31 October 1780 still gave North a comfortable majority.

The most remarkable of the new members was William Pitt, second son of the Earl of Chatham. Pitt began as a Whig and always described himself as such. He was only twenty-one, but his first speech marked him as one of the most brilliant men in Parliament. Pitt lacked his father's wrath and passion; he was Chatham's son but he was also George Grenville's nephew, and the Grenville side in him was probably stronger than that of Pitt. He was meticulous, a master of figures, calm and lucid but, unlike Grenville, he had a good idea of tact and of what was politically expedient. On 3 June 1781 he attacked North's accounts and reduced his argument to tatters. There was only one man who could match Pitt and that was Charles James Fox, but Fox was a libertine who had already gambled away one large fortune. At the moment Pitt was achieving his triumph, Fox's house in St James's Street was being taken over by the bailiffs.

Victory against France and Spain did not compensate for losses in America. A French fleet in Chesapeake Bay prevented a British squadron at New York going to the assistance of Lord Cornwallis's army in Carolina. On 19 October 1781 Cornwallis surrendered to General Washington at Yorktown on the James River. After that it was simply a question of time before American independence was accepted as an established fact. When North heard the news of the surrender, he paced up and down his study in Downing Street muttering to himself 'Oh God! it is all over!' The King showed greater self control; the only indication of his feelings was that he did not follow his usual practice of noting the precise time of despatch in his letters to the Prime Minister.

George opened Parliament on 27 November 1781 and re-affirmed his determination to recover America. The opposition made the most of their opportunity. The King, said Fox, was an arbitrary despot who had squandered his subjects' blood and treasure in his mad lust for revenge. As for his Ministers, they were the curse of the country and the laughing stock of the world; in the end, they would have to atone for their crimes beneath the executioner's axe. Such language had not been

103

heard at Westminster since the days of the Long Parliament.

The war was costing more than was ever likely to be derived from it. The cities of London and Westminster and the West Indies merchants petitioned against its continuation. Even worse, the country gentlemen, once eager supporters of the war, now began to turn against a conflict which had already cost £70 million. The county members – men of greater standing than the representatives of pocket boroughs, mere nominees of aristocratic faction – made it clear that the government would have to be altered.

George was terrified at the prospect of the return of the Whig grandees who seemed to be able to justify every action with some constitutional precedent going back to the Middle Ages. Realising that defeat was inevitable, North resigned on 20 March 1782. For the last few weeks, he had taken a terrible battering in Parliament, but he retained his good humour to the last. On the night the Prime Minister resigned, there was an unexpected snowstorm. North was practically the only member who had ordered his carriage. As he got in, he called to his enemies who were standing in the snow: 'Good night gentlemen, you see the advantages of being in the secret.' North's troubles were not over. The King was annoyed with him for not going on to the bitter end. He said 'Remember my Lord, it is you that desert me, not I you.' George's agitation is understandable; he was now at the mercy of men who had proclaimed their hatred of him. He was so distressed that he gave orders for the royal yacht to be prepared to take him to exile in Hanover.

It is only convenient shorthand to describe the opposition as 'the Whig party'. Nothing resembling a modern political party existed in the eighteenth century. There were two factions – one headed by the Marquess of Rockingham and the other by the Earl of Shelburne. Of the two, Shelburne's was the more moderate but lacked sufficient support to form a government on its own. Rockingham would have to be Prime Minister and he would take office only on condition that American Independence was acknowledged, the influence of the Crown reduced, government contractors excluded from the House of Commons, sinecures abolished, the strictest economy practised in all departments of State and the government given complete control over all Palace appointments.

Eighteenth-century Hanover.

Whatever it may have been to the King, Rockingham's government did not represent a triumph for the people, or even for 'the rising middle class'. In all his demands for reform, Rockingham was careful to say nothing about a redistribution of seats in Parliament, a measure which would have damaged his influential supporters. In composition, the Cabinet was probably the most aristocratic of all time. Edmund Burke had been useful enough in slinging taunts at North but an Irish barrister was not regarded as a fit person to occupy a seat in the Cabinet. The vice-treasurership of Ireland was thought quite good enough for William Pitt. The offer was rejected.

When the King contemplated his new Ministers, he must have repented his harsh words to North; his only request to

Rockingham was that the outgoing Prime Minister should be given a pension. Many of the new Ministers had scores to pay off, but the sharpest animosity was between the King and Charles Fox. On 23 February 1774 George had written to North: 'That young man has so thoroughly cast off every principle of common honour and honesty, that he must become as contemptible as he is odious.' Fox had originally been a supporter of North and had held a junior position at the Admiralty. He believed that George had compelled North to treat his

RIGHT George, Prince of
Wales, a portrait painted
by Sir William Beechey
in about 1797.

junior Minister badly and force him to resign. He was
determined on revenge.

Fox took his revenge in a way that was very painful to
George – through the Prince of Wales. The King's eldest son
was a clever, intelligent and pleasant boy on whom his father
doted. Unfortunately, the atmosphere of Kew Palace and
Buckingham House was too restricted for a high-spirited boy
and produced a corresponding reaction. George was a strict
father but Queen Charlotte was prepared to indulge her son in

childhood scrapes; disagreement over the boy's upbringing is said to have produced the first serious quarrel between the King and Queen. A mixture of severity and laxity had the worst possible results. The Prince of Wales grew to hate his father and one feels that he entered into many of his dissipations not for their own sake but simply to annoy the King.

At eighteen the heir to the throne had an acknowledged mistress five years older than himself; at twenty he secured the return of a candidate hostile to North for his father's 'own' borough of Windsor. He was carried home drunk, he was arrested by the watch, his usual conversation consisted mainly of obscenities, and he introduced money-lenders and pimps into his apartments at Buckingham House. It sounds exciting compared to George III's rather dull youth but it must have been upsetting to a man who cared so much about his country and his family. The Prince simply ignored his father. The King wrote that when a hunting party had ended at a little village where there was only one post chaise, the Prince hired the vehicle and drove off 'leaving me to go home in a cart if I could find one'.

Although charges that Fox acted as the Prince of Wales's procurer are groundless, he certainly helped to increase the young man's alienation from the King. Fox's influence over the Prince of Wales was well-known. Walpole wrote:

> The Prince of Wales has thrown himself into the arms of Charles and this in the most indecent and undisguised manner. Fox lodges in St James's Street, and as soon as he rises, which is very late, has a levée of his followers, and of the members of the Gaming Club at Brooks's, all his disciples. His bristly black person and shagged breast quite open, and rarely purified by any ablutions, is wrapped in a foul linen night-gown, and his bushy hair dishevelled. In these Cynic Weeds, and with epicurean good humour, does he dictate his politics, and in this school does the heir of the Crown attend his lessons and imbibe them.

Despite their animosity against the King, the Ministers exhibited something of a split personality. Ordinary members wore day clothes in Parliament, but Ministers of the Crown were expected to wear Court dress. The appearance of Fox and Burke, not in the blue and buff uniform of the American rebels, but in laced ruffles, sword belts and perfumed wigs – a livery they had

'The Prince of Wales has thrown himself into the arms of Charles'

lately derided – caused plenty of amusement. Once in office, Rockingham found there was much to be said for royal influence when it could be used to his own advantage. Professions of hatred for tyrants were hastily forgotten; Edmund Burke described a note from George as 'the best of messages from the best of Kings'. Even Fox spoke of the 'unparalleled grace' with which the Sovereign had come forward to alleviate the suffering of his people.

The Rockingham administration never had a chance of achieving its real aim – reducing the royal power to ensure that the government would never pass from the hands of about six great families 'like the Hebrew priesthood in one tribe'. The fact that most members of the Cabinet hated each other as much or more than they disliked the King gave him room for manœuvre. Any idea that the reduction of royal power might be accompanied by a recognition of the greater importance of the middle classes was rudely shattered when the Prime Minister, Cavendish and Burke declared that any Parliamentary reform would ruin the country. Only the Duke of Richmond wanted to give the vote to more people. When a proposal for an enquiry into the representative system was put forward, it came from William Pitt, who sat on the government side of the House, but without official position. The motion was defeated.

Rockingham died suddenly on 1 July 1782. Fox – who was trying hard to be a reformed character – or his uncle, the Duke of Richmond, were both considered as possible premiers, but the choice was with the King. George called for the Earl of Shelburne, Fox resigned and returned to his old wild life. The resignation was regarded as mere sulking and George's most dangerous enemy fell sharply in public esteem. Shelburne made up his Cabinet without much difficulty and William Pitt became Chancellor of the Exchequer at the age of twenty-three. When Fox turned all his brilliance against the new Prime Minister, it seemed that George's enemies were destroying themselves.

Some of Rockingham's proposals were enacted. Parliament was given more control over the distribution of the Civil List money and a start made towards the abolition of sinecures. The new government's main task was to wind up a disastrous war. After North's resignation, the war in America was virtually abandoned. Independence was conceded on 30 November 1782 and a treaty signed between Britain, France and Spain on 20 January 1783. Under the circumstances, the loss of Minorca and one or two West Indian islands could be regarded as quite favourable terms. The King announced the independence of the American Provinces on 5 December 1782. When he had finished, he asked Lord Oxford 'Did I lower my voice when I came to that part of my speech?' It was a terrible humiliation. Catherine the Great of Russia said: 'Rather than have granted America her Independence, as my brother-monarch, King George has done, I would have fired a pistol at my own head.'

As Shelburne's majority was slender, he could not afford to antagonise the King and thus no further progress was made with Rockingham's programme. There were three main factions in Parliament – the government, one headed by Fox and the still considerable group led by North. Any combination was possible. Negotiations between Fox and Shelburne broke down and North swiftly came to terms with his fiercest critic. Fond as he was of George, North was as eager as any other politician to regain the pleasures of office. He was probably too good a judge of character to have believed that Fox's threats of the block had been in earnest. North had nothing to lose but, by linking himself with the champion of the prerogative, Fox revealed the shallowness of his democratic professions and confirmed the suspicion that his only concern was office. Fox had once said that if he ever had anything to do with any member of North's government he would 'rest satisfied to be called the most infamous of mankind'. The foresight was admirable.

The means of ejecting Shelburne were utterly cynical. In Macaulay's words, 'that nothing be wanting to the scandal the great orators who had, during seven years thundered against the war, determined to join with the authors of that war in passing a vote of censure on the peace'. At 3 am on Friday, 21 February 1783, the government was defeated by seventeen votes. The Prime Minister resigned on the Monday.

Fox and North had already agreed that the Duke of Portland should be the figure-head Prime Minister in their Government. The King did not like being dictated to and asked Pitt the Younger to try to form an administration, Pitt's opinions seemed much closer to Fox than to the King. He demanded

Portland Place

The LORD of the VINEYARD.

Says the Badger to Fox,
We're in the right Box,
These Grapes are most charming & fine;

C.J.FOX

Dear Badger you're right,
We'l hem fast squeeze them tight,
And we'll drink of Patriotic Wine.

D. of Portland   L.d North

Gillray's satire on the Portland ministry of 1783. The Duke of Portland, the Lord of the Vineyard, is shown handing the grapes of office to C. J. Fox and Lord North.

reductions in taxation and the abolition of sinecures; he denounced closed boroughs and called for Parliamentary reform; he had opposed the American War and advocated independence. But Pitt was hard working and respectable to the point of priggishness – always qualities which appealed to George. At this stage, Pitt thought he would fail and declined the invitation.

111

After long negotiations George was finally forced to accept Portland as Premier with Fox and North as Secretaries of State. Fox's friends were called from the gaming tables at Brooks's and given places most of them were ill-fitted to occupy. Parliamentary reform was dropped, sinecure offices actually increased and the government contrived to pass the time by holding debates on the Book of Numbers. Consols fell and Fox, once the idol of the people, had difficulty in securing re-election to his constituency of Westminster, where all householders could vote. The political scene gave John Gillray splendid opportunities to begin his career as a cartoonist.

Fox had promised his friend the Prince of Wales that Parliament would increase his allowance to £100,000 per year – a strange aberration in a government supposedly committed to economy. The money would make the Prince independent of his father and only encourage him in his dissolute ways. George was not even consulted. When he heard of the plan, he declared that the country could not afford such extravagance – £50,000 was ample and he was prepared to pay that himself. In such a dispute, the King would have every tax payer and every parent in the country on his side. The Ministers retracted but the whole incident and the tantrums it produced had been very distressing. The King told Lord Hertford that every morning he wished himself eighty or ninety or dead.

Fox was determined not to allow George to repeat his success. On 17 November 1783 the government introduced 'A Plan for the better government of the King's East India dominions'. The Bill had good features but its main effect would be to transfer the vast patronage resources of the East India Company to Fox's nominees. The measure would have given the government so much 'pulling power' that it would be able to count on a majority for practically all time. The Bill alienated the powerful East India Company and the merchant community generally. Organisations like the Bank of England, enjoying special rights, realised that unless they used their influence against the Bill, it might be their turn next.

George saw his opportunity to strike back. A few months earlier he had been execrated by the country but now he was more popular than his Ministers. The merchants were joined by the country gentlemen who felt that the royal prerogative had been invaded for the worst possible reasons. They believed in a mixed constitution; King, Government, Parliament and Country – all had rights, but any section which sought to monopolise power would have to be taught a lesson. By now, George knew how to exploit such feelings. He saw Earl Temple, son of his old antagonist George Grenville, and gave him written authority to tell peers that their Sovereign regarded the India Bill as pernicious and would consider anyone who voted for it as a personal enemy.

The message made a great impression. Parliament was not just the preserve of Ministers; Fox had used Parliament against the King but there was nothing to stop George using the same weapon against the government. In modern times, no sovereign can intrigue so blatantly against his official servants, but in 1783 few people really regarded the King's action as unconstitutional. Such was the respect for the Crown that the mere prospect of the King's wrath reduced strong men to tears.

The King went hunting with the royal stag hounds on 18 December 1783, but it was clear that his mind was not on the chase and that he was in an agony of suspense. At length, a horseman arrived and gave George a letter. The King read it, threw out his arms and shouted 'Thank God! It is all over. The House has thrown out the Bill so there is an end of Mr Fox!' It was not quite the end. The government would not resign, so George had to send out letters of dismissal. He was so eager for his freedom that he sent out the messengers at 1 am to insist that the outgoing Ministers should give up their seals at once. Lord North was as unruffled as ever. He was in bed and asleep when Sir Evan Nepean arrived. He took his time to wake up and then refused to get out of bed to receive the King's messenger. He rang for a servant to take Nepean to his strong-room and then turned over and went back to sleep. A few hours later, William Pitt became Prime Minister at the age of twenty-four. The King had achieved a remarkable victory and secured the services of a remarkable man.

'So there is an end of Mr Fox'

Pitt appeared as the King's deliverer, much as North had been fourteen years earlier. The first months were difficult and the new Prime Minister required assistance. Between December 1783 and March 1784, the government was defeated no less than sixteen times, but the King would not hear of resignation. George had vindicated his right to choose his own Ministers but they could not go on indefinitely against a hostile Parliament. The King wanted an immediate election, but Pitt believed that the longer he waited, the larger would be his majority. There was much to attract the country gentlemen and the middle classes to an administration which really fulfilled its promises of efficiency, firmness and economy. Gradually the majorities against the government dwindled; sensible men changed sides.

The ex-Ministers used the most extreme language. Fox compared George's behaviour over the India Bill to that of the Emperor Tiberius who ordered the Senate to condemn Sejanus to death without a trial. Pamphleteers produced the most improbable stories – for example that Pitt was Queen Charlotte's lover. Such attacks actually helped the King and his protégé. Even if Fox believed his own theories – which was always doubtful – the country had not yet accepted them and did not approve of such disrespect to an anointed King. Addresses poured in thanking the King for dismissing the previous government; there was even one from Banbury, North's own pocket borough. Pitt's popularity was increased by a vicious attack on him as he was walking by Brooks's Club. Fox was accused of taking part, but explained that he could not have been involved as he had been in bed with a Mrs Armstead at the time. The explanation did not raise him in George's opinion.

When Parliament was dissolved on 25 March 1784, Pitt could count on success in the coming elections. The King was properly grateful. He wrote to Pitt 'I shall ever reflect that by the prudence, as well as the rectitude of *one* person in the House of Commons, this great change had been effected.' The elections surpassed George's most sanguine expectations. Counties turned against Foxite landowners and Fox himself had a narrow escape at Westminster, despite the support of the Prince of Wales and the efforts of the Duchess of Devonshire who went out canvassing at eight in the morning and rewarded with kisses those who promised to vote for her friend. At Dover, the sailors roasted foxes alive to show what they thought of the King's enemy. The old reprobate John Wilkes was returned as a government supporter.

Although Pitt was an able helper, much of the triumph was George's own. For nearly twenty-five years he had battled with an oligarchy which had dictated to George I and George II. The power to crush them was always latent in the Crown but it needed a politician of consummate skill to use that power to bring about the desired result.

Pitt's ascendancy meant that George could withdraw from politics much as he had done in the happier days of North's premiership. The new Prime Minister did not share his master's opinions on many points but, unlike North, he had not been the leader of a recognised faction at the time of taking office. The King had made him more than any Prime Minister since Bute and was quite capable of unmaking him. The Ministers might initiate legislation but the King had an effective veto. In his political theory and underlying awe of the Sovereign, Pitt was like most Englishmen. Even when he suffered from it, he never questioned George's right to choose his own Ministers.

The King soon recovered his good humour. He supervised improvements at Windsor and Kew and began to meet his humbler subjects more frequently. He enjoyed race meetings and visiting the country houses of his friends. In October 1785 he went to visit Lord Harcourt at Nuneham Courtenay and then proceeded on to Oxford. There were children's parties and readings by Mrs Siddons at Buckingham House. The excessive prudery of the 1760s disappeared and Mrs Siddons was often asked to read pleasantly ribald, earthy comedies like *The Provoked Husband* by Vanbrugh and Cibber.

The one thing that really distressed the King was the continuing feud with the Prince of Wales. George was never an indulgent parent and may have broken with his eldest son while there was still a chance that the boy would grow out of his wild behaviour. Unfortunately, the King could not behave like any other father; the Prince's conduct had political consequences. Fox had so antagonised George that his only hope of office was the accession of the Prince of Wales. There had been

117

The Election of 1784

In March 1784, Parliament was
dissolved and a general election was
held. Fox's popularity was at a nadir
and he was forced to fight hard to
hold on to his own seat at Westminster. Westminster was a 'scot
and lot' borough, which meant that
every male householder had the
right to vote. Thus Fox could not
depend upon patronage and
intimidation to retain the seat.

RIGHT Fox was helped in his fight
by the Duchess of Devonshire, who
went out canvassing and rewarded
promised support with kisses.

THE TWO PATRIOTIC DUCHESS'S ON THEIR CANVASS.
Requesting the favour of an early Poll.

LEFT The election of 1784, by Dighton,
with St Paul's and the hustings in the background.
ABOVE Fox standing on the hustings before St Paul's
Church in Covent Garden. The names on the hustings
refer to the wards within the constituency.

119

the same problem between George II and Frederick, but that was never accompanied by quite the same bitterness. In modern terms, the Prince had an income worth about £500,000 a year. Parental lectures on economy may irritate all young men, but a halt has to be called somewhere, and the Prince's claim that he could not live in a manner befitting his position with an income of anything less than twice the size of his present allowance was ludicrous for a single man.

A division between father and son was dangerous to the government, and Pitt was enough of a politician to desire to be on good terms with the next King. Through Lord Malmesbury, he proposed various schemes to increase the young man's already over-generous allowance. The proposals were rejected on the grounds that 'I cannot abandon Charles [Fox] and my friends'. Under Fox's influence, the heir to the throne came to believe that the King had always hated him – an absurd idea. The situation goes a long way to explain George's attitude to Fox who, whatever he may have said in public, was always far more respectful and agreeable to the King in private than the terrible George Grenville had been.

George suggested that his son should marry and the Parliament would increase his income and pay his debts. Even Fox was taken aback at the Prince's rejection of these proposals. The heir to the throne had already found the woman he wanted to marry, a rather strait-laced Roman Catholic widow named Maria Fitzherbert, who was six years older than himself. The Prince's choice was rather surprising and suggests that in all his loose-living he was really looking for a mother figure. The Prince's behaviour was in sharp contrast to that of his father in giving up his own youthful 'indiscretion'. In a way 'Prinny' behaved better; he accepted Mrs Fitzherbert's refusal to become his mistress and actually stabbed himself – though not very deeply – when she said she would not be his wife. They were married on 21 December 1785. There were two possible conclusions; either the marriage was invalid under the Royal Marriages Act, or it was legal and, under the terms of the Act of Settlement, excluded the Prince and his children from the throne.

The marriage was secret but, within three months, questions were being asked about it in Parliament. Fox had been deceived

OPPOSITE The Prince of Wales and Mrs Fitzherbert were married on 21 December 1785. This cartoon shows George III entering his son's bedroom with the document forbidding the marriage of princes of the blood without his consent. On the wall hangs a portrait of C. J. Fox, who was popularly supposed to have connived at the marriage.

120

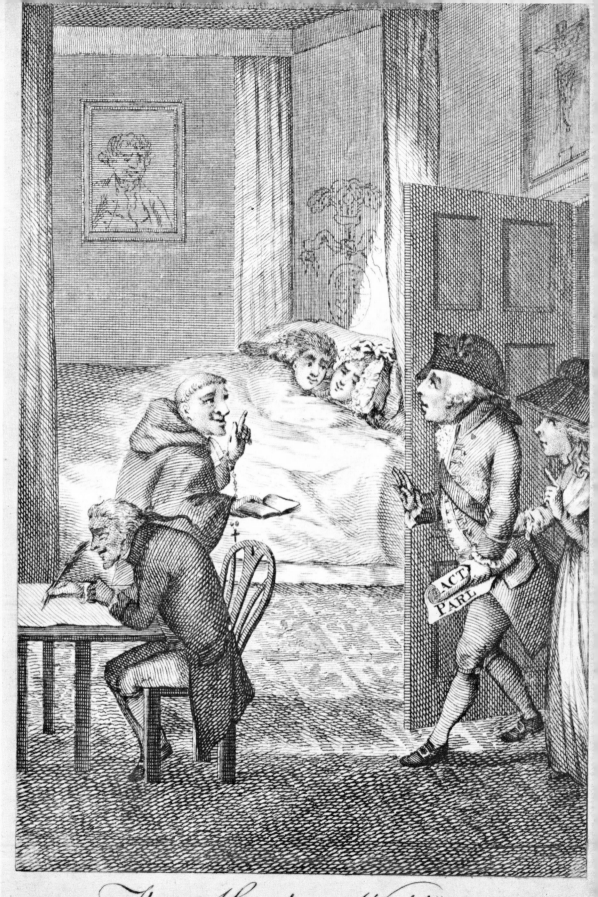

The Humbug Wedding

by his friend into thinking that the marriage had not taken place and consequently dismissed the rumour as a 'low, malicious falsehood'. At the same time, the Prince told his new wife that Fox had known and that his denial had been made to hurt her. The episode demonstrates how completely untrustworthy the Prince of Wales had become. Pitt had a much more reliable patron than Fox.

When George IV was dying, he sent for a miniature of Mrs Fitzherbert but, in life, he soon forsook her for Lady Jersey, a woman who was already the mother of five children. He gave his wife no money and actually 'borrowed' from her. George III was much kinder; despite his reputation for rigid morality, he did not treat Mrs Fitzherbert as an adventuress who had imperilled the Crown. She did not exploit her position, the King was grateful and arranged for her to receive an annuity of £6,000 for the rest of her life. Perhaps this was just to keep her quiet, but there was a real understanding of what the poor woman had to go through. Although her husband rejected her, her father-in-law always treated her as if she were his own daughter. Charges of bigamy against George III are false, those against his son are irrefutable.

According to Dr Johnson, George III's manners were quite as polished as those of Charles II or Louis XIV. Years of experience had taught him how to behave in difficult circumstances and how to use the formality of the Court to cover the embarrassments of those who knew that, in his heart, the King did not wish to see them at all. George had refused on several occasions to receive an official representative of 'that revolted state' the United States – but an interview with John Adams was finally fixed for 1 June 1785. It must have been an ordeal for Adams. At St James's Palace, he was just stared at by the assembled bishops, peers and ministers; no one spoke to him. The King was more unbending. Rather to George's surprise, Adams did the right thing of making three bows – one at the door, another halfway into the room and a third before the throne. George realised that the time had come for reconciliation. He told Adams:

> I wish you, Sir, to believe that I have done nothing in the late contest but what I thought myself indispensably bound to do by the duty which I owed my people. I was the last to consent to the

Fanny Burney, the diarist and novelist. This portrait was painted by her cousin E. F. Burney.

separation, but the separation having been made and having become inevitable, I have always said that I would be the first to meet the friendship of the United States as an independent power.

The last statement was not strictly true but it did help to break the ice.

The King was very gracious to his own subjects. The Royal Family continued to visit old Mrs Delany and persuaded her to accept a house in Windsor which the King furnished at his own expense. On certain evenings, Mrs Delany would go to the Castle where the family sat around one large table, some sewing, some reading and some drawing. The novelist Fanny Burney often stayed with Mrs Delany, but she had not been presented

123

at Court and was not supposed to meet the King in ordinary society. One evening George called unexpectedly. 'The door of the Drawing Room was opened, and a large man in deep mourning appeared at it, entering and shutting it himself without speaking. A ghost could not more have scared me when I discovered by its glitter on the black, a star!' Everyone who had not been presented tried to run away, but George told them to stay. Fanny Burney was so nervous as to be incapable of coherent conversation. Gradually the King brought things round to discuss her novel *Evelina*. Later, Miss Burney, officially Second Keeper of the Robes to the Queen, became a sort of propagandist for the domestic virtues of the Royal Family. They certainly needed something to balance the effect created by the Prince of Wales. Fanny Burney developed a high regard for the Queen and was surprised to find her an extremely well-read woman.

The Thames-side Palladian villa of Nuneham Park in Oxfordshire, which stands in a landscape setting created by Capability Brown. The King and his Court first visited Nuneham in 1785 to stay with Lord Harcourt.

Apart from the conduct of the Prince of Wales, domestic life was happy. George fretted that his third son, the future William IV, might be ensnared by the daughter of his commanding officer at Portsmouth. All the younger members of the family caught whooping cough and three of the boys, Ernest, Augustus and Adolphus, were sent off to study at the university of

Göttingen. Great care was always taken to preserve the German connection and Madame Schwellenberg, the Queen's confidante, was suspected of having some political influence.

The King was more popular than ever before, the government in capable hands, trade booming and the confidence destroyed during the American War fast returning. The King responded to this more exuberant mood. In February 1786 Mrs Siddons was called to Buckingham House to take the part of Mrs Lovemore in Murphy's comedy *The Way to Keep Him*. A few days later, Mrs Billington sang for the first time in London, taking the part of Rosetta in Bickerstaffe's opera *Love in a Village*. George did much to encourage her career.

There were more parties on the terrace at Windsor in honour of the children's birthdays. But not all domestic arrangements went smoothly. A visit to Nuneham may have delighted the King, but it was not to charm the rest of the Court who disliked the 'straggling, half new, half old, half comfortable, half forlorn mansion' and the offhand treatment they received from 'prodigious fine yellow laced menials'. Fanny Burney and the royal governess nearly fainted with horror when they were expected to eat at a common supper table with the higher servants and summoned to dinner by a footman bellowing 'The Equerries want the ladies.' If life on a royal tour was uncomfortable for ladies like Fanny Burney, it must have been much worse for the real servants but, unfortunately, they did not record their experiences.

Lack of political pressure gave the King more time to assist worthy causes, such as Sunday Schools and prison reform. Above all, George now had the leisure to develop his knowledge of botany into a real expertise on agricultural questions. He wrote several pamphlets under the name of Ralph Robinson. Some of Richmond New Park was turned into arable land and the King exercised personal supervision over the running of the deer park. George was partly responsible for the formation of the General Board of Agriculture which did much to improve productivity and yields – so necessary at a time of rapid population growth, the expansion of towns and the beginnings of industrialisation. Royal fashions caught on quickly; great improving landlords like the Duke of Bedford and Coke of Norfolk owed much to the King's example.

The Georgian Country House

The two great country-house architects of the late eighteenth century were Robert Adam and James Wyatt. Adam had visited Italy in the 1750s to study not Palladio, as had his predecessors, but Imperial Roman architecture. He returned with a large repertoire of antique ornaments which he was to adapt and use with unsurpassed brilliance. He designed many great houses including Kedleston, Osterley and Syon.

James Wyatt, on the other hand, was the great proponent of Palladianism of this period. His houses include the interior of Chatsworth, Doddington House and Heveningham Hall. At Heveningham he produced a series of magnificent Palladian rooms for Sir Gerard Vanneck.

ABOVE LEFT Drawing by Robert Adam for the interior of Home House in Portman Square, St Marylebone.

ABOVE The central section of the Adam ceiling in the Ballroom at Home House, which is now part of the Courtauld Institute of Art.

LEFT The Library at Heveningham Hall, Suffolk. For the interior Wyatt used soft delicate colours as background, on which he applied in paint and low plaster relief pictures 'from the antique' to give elegance and repose.

'Coke of Norfolk', member of Parliament for Norfolk and a great agriculturalist. He introduced many improvements into his estates at Holkham, enabling wheat to be grown in the area for the first time, and for improved breeds of sheep, cattle and pigs to be raised. His great Palladian house of Holkham can be seen in the background of the picture.

On 2 August 1786 George was getting out of his carriage at the garden entrance to St James's Palace when a well-dressed woman pushed her way out of the crowd and held out a paper to the King; suddenly she took out a knife and tried to stab him in the chest. Fortunately, the weapon was so worn and thin that it bent on George's waistcoat. The woman, Margaret Nicholson, was disarmed and the surrounding crowd seemed likely to tear her limb from limb. The King interposed 'The poor creature is mad; do not hurt her; She has not hurt me.' Margaret Nicholson was the daughter of a barber from Stockton-on-Tees who believed that the crown was hers by right and that if it were denied her, England would be 'deluged in blood for a thousand years'. When asked on what grounds she made her claim, she replied that it was a mystery. To George's relief, she was declared insane and not executed for treason. When the King next appeared in public everyone seemed full of en-

thusiasm. With some shrewdness he observed that the increase in popularity made up for any danger he had been in.

Relations between the Prince of Wales and his father improved. After the King had increased his son's allowance, the two met for three hours at Buckingham House on 25 May 1787. There was a reconciliation and the Prince said he was sorry for his past faults and, in the next few weeks, appeared in public frequently with his father. Even better for the King, the Duke of York was returning from Germany, apparently uninfluenced by the bad example set by his elder brother. As the boy emerged from his coach in the quadrangle at Windsor Castle, his sub-governor declared 'It was not pleasure that beamed in the King's eye, it was *ecstacy*.' At least the Prince of Wales was not jealous of his father's love for his younger brother; he broke off his engagements at Brighton and hurried to Windsor for a general family reunion. It was all too good to last.

George III enjoyed sketching and painting. This illustration is one of his watercolours of Syon House, the Adam mansion of the Dukes of Northumberland in Middlesex.

6
Madness
1787-8

THE PRINCE OF WALES soon returned to his old tricks of obstructing his father's ministers – even to the extent of over-priming Sir James Erskine with brandy in the House of Commons coffee room, so that the great lawyer disgraced himself by running riot against the government and making obscene comments on Pitt. The really disturbing development was that the Duke of York now followed his brother into debauchery. He began a liaison with the Countess of Tyrconnell, a lady whom Mrs Fitzherbert declined to receive on the grounds that she was 'contaminate'.

All this, no doubt, distressed the King, but he had faced worse troubles before and emerged triumphant. He had enjoyed excellent health for twenty years and was probably fitter than the Prince of Wales. He may have been too self-disciplined but there is plenty of evidence that he could relax. Various psychological explanations have been given for the mental illness which he developed in the autumn of 1788. Some emphasise the importance of his over-dominant mother (who had been dead sixteen years); some stress his resentment that he was not allowed to marry Lady Sarah Lennox and suggest that, subconsciously, he hated his wife; others think that he must have been a strange man anyway because he did not take advantage of the available opportunities. Lady Anne Hamilton, as ever, had a scandalous and unlikely explanation; she thought that the illness was caused by George's guilt about his bigamy and triggered off by the pregnancy of one of his daughters. When one or several of these considerations are added to the pressures of kingship, the whole thing is regarded as obvious. Calm in the face of crisis becomes merely the bottling up of emotion which, one day, was bound to explode. The King, claim many writers, might have done very well as a country squire, but he was not tough enough for the Crown.

None of these explanations is convincing. The long period of health between 1765 and 1788 is puzzling and the psychological conclusions find it hard to account for the physical symptoms which preceded the onset of madness by some weeks. It is possible that these symptoms were merely hysterical, but they did follow a precise pattern which suggests that they ought to be taken more seriously than has been usual in George's biographies.

PREVIOUS PAGES
The behaviour of the Prince of Wales concerning his father's madness was frequently thoughtless and occasionally cruel. Rowlandson's cartoon of the 1788 Regency crisis shows the Prince with his drunken companions, Richard Brindsley Sheridan and Colonel George Hanger, bursting into his father's bedroom

BELOW Sir George Baker, the King's physician.

Despite his modest diet, the King suffered a series of bilious attacks in June 1788. It was thought that his Germanic taste for sauerkraut had not helped. The trouble soon cleared but George's own doctor, Sir George Baker, suggested that he should take the waters at Cheltenham – essentially a mixture of Glauber and Epsom salts whose general effect was purgative. The Court left Windsor for Bays Hill Lodge, just outside Cheltenham, on 12 July 1788. The King took the waters at six in the morning and then promenaded in the Walks with the Queen and his daughters. He made various excursions from Cheltenham – to see the Earl of Bathurst at Oakley, to Glouces- ter Cathedral, to Tewkesbury Abbey and to Worcester, where he was entertained by his old friend Bishop Hurd and attended the Three Choirs Festival. Even the Duke of York came down for a day.

The tour was a great success. There were no guards, in every town huge crowds came to see the King, and the Royal Family could scarcely go five miles without meeting a country band playing 'God Save the King'. George enjoyed himself enor- mously and spoke to anyone he met. On one of his rides, he overtook a farmer driving sheep:

> His Majesty rode with him a quarter of an hour, conversing upon the value and properties of the land, the prices of sheep and cattle

In July 1788, the Royal family visited Cheltenham to take the waters. This cartoon shows the King drinking the waters, but being pulled away by Queen Charlotte.

... the farmer grown familiar asked the gentleman, as he thought, if he had seen the King; and being answered in the affirmative, the farmer said 'Our neighbours say he's a good sort of man, but dresses very plain.' 'Aye' said His Majesty 'as *plain* as you see me now,' and rode on.

The King returned to Kew apparently better. He suffered from slight constipation and experienced pains in his face which made it difficult to sleep. No one thought there was anything serious. On 16 October 1788 George went riding in the rain and did not change his stockings when he came in. Sir Gilbert Elliot wrote to his wife.

> The King was unwell all the evening, and went to bed at his usual hour. About one in the morning he was seized violently with a cramp or some other violent thing in the stomach, which rendered him speechless, and in a word was *all but*. The Queen ran out in great alarm, in her *shift,* or with very little clothes, among the pages, who, seeing her in that situation, were at first retiring out of respect, but the Queen stopped them and sent them instantly for the Apothecary at Richmond who arrived in about forty minutes, during which time the King had continued in the fit and speechless. The Apothecary tried to make him swallow something strong, but the King still liked a bit of his own way, and rejected by signs everything of the sort. They contrived, however, to cheat him and got some cordial down in the shape of medicine, and the fit went off.

The fact that 'the Apothecary at Richmond' who took forty minutes to arrive was thought sufficient gives some idea of the general estimate of the King's health. The next day, a rash appeared on George's back which looked as if it had been scourged; his eyes became yellow and his urine very dark. On 19 October these symptoms disappeared, although the feet were swollen and painful. There were no signs of mental disturbance until 22 October; even these can be attributed to the opium-based drugs administered to the patient. George's eyes looked wild and he told Baker that the importation of senna ought to be prohibited. Repeating himself constantly, he went on in the same vein for three hours.

A levée was due for 24 October. Pitt did not want to create alarm and George wished to keep his illness a secret. He appeared, his legs wrapped in flannel, and the levée passed without mishap. Afterwards, however, when Lord Chancellor Thurlow advised the King to go to Windsor, he received a strange reply: 'You too, then, my Lord Thurlow, forsake me and suppose me ill beyond recovery; but whatever you and Mr Pitt may think and feel, I, *that am born a gentleman* shall never lay my head on my last pillow in peace and quiet so long as I remember the loss of my American colonies.' Although George was in pain, the interview was conducted with both parties standing – a curious innovation into English Court etiquette imported by the King from Germany. As discussions often lasted three hours, the custom can scarcely have helped either monarch or Ministers to concentrate on the country's problems.

When the King returned to Windsor, he startled Fanny Burney by the hoarseness of his voice and extreme volubility. The illness followed almost exactly the course of 1765; his pulse raced, his speech was extremely rapid and his eyesight and hearing deteriorated. The former lover of music could not bear to hear it. George did his best to save his family from distress. It was not easy; he had a desire to talk ceaselessly which was difficult to control. Occasionally some of his anguish was revealed. He told his friend Lady Effingham that he had become an old man all at once. He was weak and needed a stick to support himself. But George's fear was more terrible than age. Long before most of his doctors, the King believed he was going mad. It was a terrible prospect for any man. He recovered sufficiently by the beginning of November to go riding with the Duke of York; suddenly he burst into tears and said he would prefer death to insanity. One day the Queen tried to comfort her husband by saying that everyone should bear up under affliction; he put his arm round her and said 'Then you are prepared for the worst.'

About this time, the famous incident of George and the oak tree is alleged to have occurred. The story first appeared in a pamphlet entitled *A History of the Royal Malady,* which was published some eight months later, in the summer of 1789. The author was Philip Withers, a senior page of the Presence who was dismissed from the King's service in April 1789. Withers certainly had a grudge against the Royal Family and many of his stories, such as the King indecently assaulting one of his wife's maids, was admittedly at fourth hand. Withers claimed

'You are prepared for the worst'

to have been present at the oak tree incident but his story must be treated with caution. The King and Queen were riding in Windsor Great Park; Withers continued,

> His Majesty now approached a venerable oak that had enlivened the solitude of that quarter of the park for upwards of a century and a half. At the distance of a few yards, he uncovered [i.e. took off his hat] and advanced, bowing with the utmost respect, and then seizing one of the lower branches, he shook it with the most apparent cordiality and regard just as a man shakes his friend by the hand. ... On my approach, I perceived that the King was engaged in earnest conversation. Perhaps the learned may censure the term – Conversation – as properly implying alternate intercourse of ideas. And yet I humbly conceive the Converse of the objection is in force against the term – Soloquy; for his Majesty anticipated the answer of his royal Friend and then made a reply.
>
> It was the King of Prussia to whom his Majesty gave this rural interview. Continental politics were the subject. What I heard it would be unpardonable to divulhe. I cannot however withhold a remark that must fill every loyal bosom with pleasure. His Majesty, though under a momentary dereliction of reason, evinced the most cordial attachment to Freedom and the Protestant Faith.

George's self control relaxed in the evenings and he talked ceaselessly. At dinner on 5 November obvious madness appeared for the first time. The Queen had hysterics and even the worldly Prince of Wales was in tears. Charlotte said her husband's eyes looked like black currant jelly; he spoke nonsense and foam ran out of his mouth. During the meal George attacked the Prince of Wales and tried to smash his head against the wall. That night the King was put in a room next to the Queen's but no one dared to place guards to see that he did not become violent. George thought Charlotte was going to be taken away from him and went to her room to see if she was still there. The Queen believed she was going to be murdered.

Next morning Baker and his assistants thought that the King would not live; even if he survived, it was unlikely that he would recover his reason. The Prince of Wales sent his own medical adviser, Dr Warren, whose prognosis was even gloomier. A new reign seemed only a matter of days away. When the Bishop of Lincoln called upon Pitt, he found the Prime Minister waiting for news of George's death. In more

136

sensible moments, the King locked up his papers and jewels except his watch and a picture of the Queen. He told his German page Ernst that he would soon die; his only amusement was to go through the Court calendar marking the names of people he intended to dismiss.

Doctors thought that 'a gouty humour' had settled in the King's brain and gave him James's powder to sweat it out. They had no success. On 9 November there was a rumour in London that the King was dead. The Prince of Wales took charge of everything and the Queen retired to just two rooms in Windsor Castle. George survived the crisis but his sanity showed no signs of returning. His equerry, Robert Fulke Greville, described his condition on 12 November:

> In the morning, constant rambling of thought continued, yet still at times recollecting Persons around him by name. About 3 o'clock this day he became more violent and his talking was hurried and agitated to a great degree, and in consequence he put himself in a violent perspiration. At this time, his pulse rose to 130 but at 5 o'clock this evening, His Majesty became exceedingly turbulent and made strong efforts to get out of bed. His exertions with great agitation of words continued about an hour. He afterwards became more composed but the rambling remained.

Observers were reluctant to record what a much-respected King said in his ravings. Sometimes George declared himself in love with Lady Pembroke, a grandmother well over fifty, and on other occasions said that the institution of marriage would soon be abolished. These examples seem to support the 're-pressed sexuality' argument, but it is hard to apply the same interpretation to most of the things George said. He declared he could see Hanover through Herschel's telescope; he thought London had been flooded and expressed anxiety about a valuable manuscript he had left there; he issued apparently sensible orders but applying to people who did not exist. As the King's strength returned, he invented various stratagems to thwart those he regarded as his gaolers. By 19 November he had a fortnight's growth of beard; he allowed one side of his face to be shaved, but then refused to let the barber continue unless he received guarantees of greater freedom. Coercion became necessary and on 20 November George Selwyn wrote:

Dr Warren, the medical adviser to the Prince of Wales.

Dr Warren in some set of fine phrases is to tell his Majesty that he is stark mad and must have a strait waistcoat. I am glad that I am not chosen to be that Rat who is to put the Bell about the Cat's neck. For if it should please God to restore his Majesty to his senses, I should not like to stand in the place of that man who has moved such an Address to the Crown.

Windsor was too much in the public gaze and it was decided to transfer the King to Kew. Various deceptions, notably that he would be allowed to see the Queen, had to be employed to persuade George to travel. Kew was far from ideal. It was a summer palace; there were not enough fire-places for winter use, many of the rooms had no carpets, and sandbags had to be put against the windows to keep out the draughts. When George discovered he had been tricked, he became increasingly violent, attacked his pages and refused his medicine.

George's main doctor at Kew was Dr Francis Willis of Lincoln. The King's ordinary doctors had little experience of mental illness. Willis kept a private lunatic asylum; he was considered an expert in his field but regarded as a quack by the royal doctors because he was not a member of the College of Physicians. Willis was not unqualified and had a degree in medicine from the University of Oxford. In his first interview with Willis, George displayed a biting wit which the Doctor put down to madness but sounds very much like the return of sanity. The King said to him 'Sir, Your dress and appearance bespeak you of the Church, do you belong to it?' Willis replied that he had given up preaching for medicine and added 'Our Saviour himself went about healing the sick.' 'Yes, yes,' said the King 'but He had not £700 a year for it.'

Willis compared his methods with the insane to the way in which wild horses are 'broken in'. Lectures, threats and the strait-jacket played a large part in his treatment. If the King refused food or was restless, his legs were tied to the bed and a band strapped across his chest. Later Willis introduced a special chair to restrain his patient; with bitter irony George called it his 'Coronation Chair'. If the King objected to anything, his mouth was gagged; he was denied the use of a knife and fork. Willis's assistants were unnecessarily brutal and Ernst sometimes struck and mocked his master. Willis's treatment was not far

Dr Francis Willis, the King's principal doctor at Kew. He was brought in to deal with the King because of his experience with mental illness, but his methods were brutal and catastrophic.

removed from the days when mental illness was regarded as possession by devils and the only way to cure it was by tormenting the evil spirit – and thus the patient – to persuade him to go elsewhere. If Willis's views were not quite so crude, at the root of his attitude was a belief that madness was a sign of sin and should be punished as such. Although George recovered in time in Willis's care there is no evidence that the treatment helped; it only made the poor man more confused and delayed his return to health.

The Treatment of Lunatics

The treatment of mental illness in the eighteenth
century had hardly advanced from the medieval
belief that attributed insanity to possession by
devils. Thus the devils must be forced to leave the
possessed by tormenting them. If this did not work,
then the mentally ill were isolated and fettered to
prevent them from doing harm to others.

BELOW William Norris, an inmate of Bedlam
Hospital for fourteen years. His movements were
restricted by chains around his arms, legs and neck,
but his sole crime had been attempted escape from
the asylum.

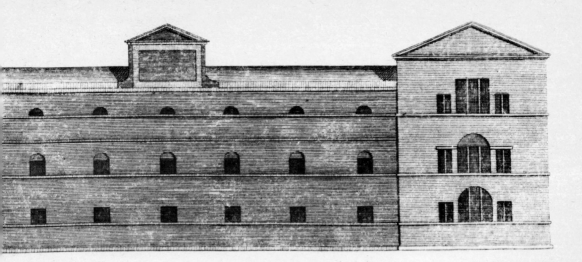

ABOVE St Luke's Hospital
in Moorfields from Stow's
Survey of London.
LEFT 'Scene in Bedlam'
from Hogarth's
Rake's Progress.

George was not helped by quarrels among the royal doctors. Willis was treating him for a psychological illness while Warren and Baker believed that he was suffering from a physical disease which caused mental aberrations. Their diagnosis was correct and at least they opposed Willis's barbarous treatment; unfortunately their own remedies did no more good. Warren insisted on blistering George's feet and legs with powdered Spanish Fly and mustard plasters in an attempt to draw out the 'ill humour'. Warren thought the wounds 'discharged well' but in reality he had only succeeded in creating an infection in limbs which were already painful. The King was in agony and tried to rip off the terrible plasters. He might have recovered quicker if he had succeeded, but he was restrained and put back in the strait jacket.

Despite the efforts of Warren and Willis, George began to recover about Christmas time. He played backgammon with Willis, saw the Queen and made arrangements with a jeweller to give gold watches to his attendants. On 17 February 1789 the King was said to be convalescent but Willis stayed on for another month to see there was no relapse. George had lost three stone in weight during his illness, his face looked 'as sharp as a knife' and his eyes appeared more prominent than before. On 3 March he was thought safe enough to sleep in the Queen's bed and a week later his recovery was officially announced by the Lord Chancellor. He returned to Windsor and on 23 April attended a three-hour service in St Paul's Cathedral to celebrate his recovery. When the Archbishop of Canterbury said that the strain might be too much, George replied 'I have twice read over the evidence of the physicians in my case, and if I can stand that, I can stand anything.' Only the sound of five thousand children singing affected the King's nerves in any way during the celebrations to mark his return to health. Apart from some minor stomach trouble in 1795, the King was well for another twelve years.

Doctors were utterly confused by the King's illness. Hosts of theories were produced and remedies suggested. Until recently historians have believed those who advanced a psychological explanation. Many biographies assumed, wrongly, that George must have been mad in 1765; from there it was only a short step to implying that he must have been mad all his life. The whole

142

effect has been to produce a distorted picture of the man and thus of his importance as an active and successful politician.

George III suffered from porphyria, a disturbance of the porphyrin metabolism. This is the process which produces the pigments which give blood its red colour. If there is more of the pigment in the body than is needed by the blood, the urine becomes discoloured and the whole nervous system, including the brain, is poisoned. Porphyria can exist in varying degrees of severity; delirium only occurs in extreme cases and it is possible for the same person to have attacks which vary in intensity. The real clue to porphyria is red urine, which can be distinguished from that simply affected by blood by the very rapid changes of colour from normal to almost purple and back again, perhaps several 'cycles' within one day. The misplaced delicacy of early biographies in omitting this crucial symptom has helped to lead later writers astray.

Porphyria can be transmitted from generation to generation and the diagnosis is supported by milder symptoms of the same disease appearing in other members of the King's family – his sister the Queen of Denmark, four of his sons, including George IV, and several of his German relations. The disease can be traced back at least as far as Mary Queen of Scots and her son James I. James had porphyria nearly as badly as George and suffered from spells of delirium. His symptoms were almost identical to those of his direct descendant – except that in James's case the features of his illness were recorded far more accurately. James's Swiss doctor, Sir Theodore de Mayerne, came much closer to an understanding of the complaint than any of the medical men a century and a half later. James also suffered less pain – if only because he refused medical attention. He may have been regarded as a fool but Mayerne's comment, 'the King laughs at medicine and holds it so cheap that he declares physicians of very little use and hardly necessary. He asserts the art of medicine to be supported by mere conjecture' was almost as true in 1789 as it had been in the 1620s.

Porphyria was not understood until the 1930s and there is still no cure – although fortunately the disease is rare. George's fear of becoming fat gave him the wrong idea that meat was bad for him; it is known that a low protein diet increases the likelihood of an attack and that cases are made worse by any infection. Dr Warren's blisters could not have been more damaging. The doctors would have done well to have given the King an occasional dose of laudanum to keep him quiet, but otherwise have left the attack to run its course.

News of the King's illness gave remarkable proof of his popularity and the poor opinion most solid citizens had of the Prince of Wales. Government stock fell sharply. It was believed that the doctors had bungled and Warren and Baker received letters threatening that if the King died they would pay for their mistakes with their lives. The Prince of Wales took control at Windsor and refused to allow many of his father's friends into the Castle. He seized George's private papers, jewels and money and, when the Queen objected, the Duke of York said 'Madam, I believe you are as much deranged as the King.' The Prince of Wales smuggled Lord Lothian into the royal apartments to hear George's ravings at their worst. Gamblers at Brooks's Club changed the name of the card usually called 'The King' to 'The Lunatic'; in the same room, the Duke of York mimicked his father in his madness.

> '*Madam, I believe you are as much deranged as the King*'

George's illness encouraged the opposition, whose hopes of office had receded further since 1784. They became so confident that they discussed the distribution of offices in the new government. Richard Brinsley Sheridan was thought to have supplanted Fox in the Prince of Wales's regard and was thus expected to be the next Premier. Even if George were to survive but remained insane, the Prince would have to be made Regent with almost all the powers of a King; he could still turn Pitt out without any fear of retribution. The Whigs naturally made the most of George's illness. The government, on the other hand, could expect nothing from the Prince of Wales. Pitt and his supporters were eager to prove that the King would recover and, thus, even if a Regency were necessary at all, the Prince would only need enough power to hold the reins for a few months.

Both sides found medical opinion to support their interests; details of the King's illness were bandied about in a most unpleasant way. Warren and Baker were 'opposition doctors' who pointedly snubbed the Queen and sent reports direct to the Prince of Wales. When the doctors were examined by a

The family of George III
in 1770. Left to right:
William, Duke of
Clarence, George Prince
of Wales, Frederick, Duke
of York, Princess Augusta,
George III, Princess
Charlotte, Princess
Elizabeth and Queen
Charlotte. Painting by
John Zoffany.

146

Parliamentary Committee, Warren insisted that the King was not delirious but insane and thus unlikely to recover. Willis, on the other hand, was equally convinced that George would ultimately regain his senses. The two sides began a smear campaign on each other's doctors. It was not an edifying spectacle.

Lord Chancellor Thurlow was in communication with the opposition and revealed details of Pitt's plans for a restricted Regency. Under the Prime Minister's scheme, the Queen was to be in control of the King's treatment and general welfare and given charge of all household matters. The Regent might appoint Ministers but he would not be able to create peers, alienate royal property or grant pensions. Without such leverage, it would be much harder to get rid of a government which was generally popular in the country. The Prince was furious; he had been advised by his friend Wedderburn, Franklin's persecutor and now Chief Justice of Common Pleas, that the Regency with all the powers of kingship was his by right and that if these rights were denied, he might lawfully seize them by force. According to Wedderburn, the affair simply did not concern Parliament; his friend should become Regent automatically. This was nonsense. The heir to the throne has no more 'right' to the Regency in the eyes of the law than any other subject. It is not a question of right; if the Sovereign is incapacitated, the appropriate arrangements are decided by Parliament.

This was a reversal of roles. Fox had been all for Parliament against the King, now he was for the Regent against Parliament. Political theories were soon forgotten when they did not square with his interests. Fox claimed that the Prince of Wales had the same rights as if the King were dead. Not only was this wrong in law but the tone of the speech caused grave offence. Seeing the way the wind was blowing, Thurlow hastily broke off his flirtation with Fox and with supreme hypocrisy declared 'When I forget my Sovereign, may my God forget me.' The only political capital Fox could make was to allege that the Queen was scheming for power at the expense of her son. Pamphleteers raked up the old story of an affair between Charlotte and Pitt, and the Prince of Wales thought – incorrectly – that his father would be angry if he ever discovered how the Prime Minister had tried to restrict 'royal' power.

'When I forget my Sovereign, may my God forget me'

The Regency Bill passed through the House of Commons on 12 February 1789. Fox and his friends would be glad of office even if it were only for a few weeks. The game of distributing offices in the 'next' government began again. George's recovery was now so rapid that it was clear that even these hopes would be disappointed. It was said that when the King became sane, Edmund Burke would go mad. Most of the Whigs just drowned their sorrows in drink.

The Prince of Wales and the Duke of York now faced the disagreeable prospect of their father calling on them to account for their behaviour during the previous three months. They decided to get their say in first and saw the King at Kew on 23 February 1789. Everything was done to flatter George, and his sons even congratulated him on using his convalescence to improve his Latin. For the next few weeks letters of affection, reverence and duty poured in; the young men made the surprising claim that their one desire had been to protect their father.

These protestations cut no ice. By the beginning of March all the Household officers who had supported the Prince of Wales during the Regency crisis had been dismissed. In a vain attempt to discredit members of the Royal Family who had remained loyal to their father, the Prince started a rumour that his sister, the Princess Royal, was pregnant. Both he and the Duke of York were in furious tempers throughout the service in St Paul's and both refused to attend galas put on by foreign embassies and London clubs to celebrate their father's recovery. The Duke of York pointedly helped to arrange a dance for the London *demi-monde* to coincide with one such occasion.

The Queen was outraged at the way in which Fox tried to exploit the King's illness. For the first time she openly emerged as a political partisan and would scarcely speak to opposition supporters. Charlotte was even more scandalised by her sons' conduct. She had never shared her husband's special affection for the Duke of York and now tried to blame him for actions which had clearly originated with the Prince of Wales. When she heard that the Duke had been challenged to a duel by the Duke of Richmond's son, Colonel Lennox, she immediately invited the Colonel to a ball at Buckingham House and made a great point of talking to him. Perhaps it was not the behaviour one would expect from a mother but there had been great provocation. At least it suggests that Charlotte was still deeply attached to her husband. The Prince of Wales complained to the King that the Queen expressed neither alarm at her son's danger nor joy at his safety. George did not take such positive steps of disapproval; very sadly he said 'It kills me, it goes to my soul, I know not how to bear it.'

After his illness, the King needed a holiday and was glad of the opportunity to meet more of his subjects. At last he was beginning to free himself from the restrictions of Court life which had once severely damaged his popularity. The tour of 1789 was an enormous success. In every village there were laurel arches, music and children throwing flowers in front of the royal party. At the edge of the New Forest, the King was met by the foresters who presented him with their traditional gift to the Sovereign – two white greyhounds wearing silver collars held by silken cords. When George was staying at Lyndhurst, Charles II's hunting lodge in the Forest, the guard was of archers in green. The King attended Lyndhurst church where the congregation insisted on singing 'God Save the King' instead of the Psalm.

The main purpose of the visit was for the King to benefit from sea-bathing at Weymouth. Sea-bathing was the latest fashion, Brighton was already being transformed by the Prince of Wales's patronage into a booming resort. Many little fishing towns were eager to enjoy the same experience. Spas, and Cheltenham in particular, took a hard knock from the King's

Sea-bathing from bathing machines at the beginning of the nineteenth century.

illness following on so shortly after he had taken the waters. There were considerations apart from genuine loyalty which guaranteed the King a tremendous welcome at Weymouth. The presence of the Court created employment for the working people, profit for the tradesmen and generally gave a tremendous boost to a town wishing to attract rich and important visitors. In the course of the summer, the visitors included the Prime Minister, the Solicitor-General and the actress Mrs Siddons. Fanny Burney was disappointed in Pitt whose appearance she considered 'neither noble nor expressive'.

George suffered minor annoyances but generally enjoyed himself. It cannot have been very pleasant to be followed into the sea by a bathing machine containing yet another band playing 'God Save the King'. The Court was scandalised when the mayor refused to kneel before his sovereign, making the feeble excuse that he had a wooden leg; the King wisely made light of the incident. From Weymouth the royal party went on to Exeter where the same welcome was waiting. At Plymouth the King visited the dockyards and watched a naval review from the frigate *Southampton*. The tour was such a success that George returned in 1791, when his great interest in the agriculture of Wiltshire and Dorset earned him the nickname of Farmer George. But meeting people was not always pleasant; in August 1791, James Sutherland, dismissed from a judicial position in Minorca – then a British possession – committed suicide in the King's presence. George was very upset.

If the outside world was not always agreeable, the Court was becoming more relaxed. After dinner on 4 June 1791 – the King's birthday – the Duke of Clarence, later William IV, entered the apartments of Madame Schwellenberg in St James's Palace. Schwellenberg was Queen Charlotte's favourite lady-in-waiting, but the rest of the Court considered her rather a dragon and called her Cerbera. The Duke had been celebrating his father's birthday and his own recent promotion to Rear Admiral. He forced the company to drink bumper after bumper of champagne to his father's health. Schwellenberg grew alarmed and said she feared that Prince William would be late for another appointment. Upon this William replied 'Hold your potato jaw my dear' and then started to kiss her hand. The next morning he told his sister Princess Mary 'You may think

Stubbs' painting of Josiah
Wedgwood and his family.
Wedgwood came from a
family of potters; he
quickly prospered and in
1762 he was appointed
potter first to the Queen
and then the King.

how far I was gone, for I kissed the Schwellenberger's hand.'
Unexpectedly the lady seemed delighted and said in her
German-English 'Dat Prince William him really very merry;
oders vat you call tipsy.'

The Royal Family seemed happier. In September 1791 the
Duke of York married a daughter of Frederick William II of
Prussia. Although the Duke was not always faithful, the marriage was quite successful and the young man's behaviour
became somewhat more sober. The Prince of Wales was
reconciled with the Queen, but quarrelled with the Duke of
York. In some ways this was a pity, but it did mean that the
brothers would no longer collaborate in tormenting their
father.

George was now over fifty and had been King for thirty
years. The early 1790s saw the death of many of the leading
figures of the early years of the reign, men who still regarded
George as a rather inexperienced young man. Both Bute and
North died in 1792. To the younger generation, the King
already seemed an old man, a fixture who had always been
there, old-fashioned and slightly out of touch, but still clever
and awesome. Things were changing in the country and some
of the younger men thought that this would have to be reflected
in a general overhaul of Parliament, the law and the machinery

of government. Few thought there was a need for anything very drastic.

So long as they were not actually starving, the people knew their places and most of the middle classes were happy to accept the *status quo*. A rich merchant could always buy himself a pocket borough so that the commercial interest was not unrepresented in Parliament. The supremacy of the aristocracy was as serene as ever. The appearance of a few cotton families was scarcely noticed. If it was, the nobility was quite as ready to profit from the new world – especially by their investment in canals – as any thrusting self-made man. There had been popular disturbances in the past but they lacked real political coherence. The most important division in politics still seemed to be between the country gentlemen and the great aristocrats – exactly as it had been in the seventeenth century.

England had a lot to be thankful for. The taxation system was unnecessarily complicated and in need of reform, but the poor carried a smaller proportion of the total burden than anywhere else in Europe. The picture of the eighteenth century as a time of heavy protective duties, 'the mercantilist age', is a myth created by Victorian free-traders. Most of the obnoxious duties were imposed for revenue purposes during the Revolutionary Wars. There was a recognition of the need for change and Pitt had concluded a successful commercial treaty with France based on free-trade ideas. In other spheres progress was disappointing. The Prime Minister favoured a redistribution of seats in Parliament, the granting of full rights to Roman Catholics and the abolition of the Slave Trade. George was not enthusiastic for any of these measures and, for the moment, they came to nothing. The King was cautious but he was not opposed to all change and many people thought that Pitt would bring him round.

In about 1792, however, there was a change from realistic conservatism to bigotted reaction in George's mind. In common with most of the political establishment, he came to believe that the slightest concession to progress would inevitably lead to anarchy. This dangerous rigidity was caused by the French Revolution. It is a pity that this picture has been accepted as the 'true' George III. Whatever it may have done for France, the Revolution was a tragedy for England.

7
Revolution and Emancipation 1788–1801

AT FIRST, Pitt hoped that revolution would give France something like an English system of government – that it would be a French 1688. Events in France produced a split in the Whig party. One section, 'the alarmists', which included Edmund Burke, quickly forgot their democratic principles when there appeared the remotest likelihood of their being implemented. Burke was soon outdoing the government in his horror at any changes in British institutions and supporting Pitt's measures to suppress any revolutionary activity in Britain. Fox, on the other hand, welcomed events across the Channel and hoped that they would act as a spur to the quest for liberty in England. Fox's sincerity is always suspect, but many of his supporters, including the future Lord Grey, genuinely believed that reform of the more obvious abuses was needed, not to precipitate but to prevent revolution.

The King's attitude was more sensible than most. He condemned both mob violence and despotic government. When a crowd of 'loyalists' smashed up a meeting in Birmingham which was discussing the advantages of democracy, George insisted that those who had broken the law must be punished. Three of the loyalists were hanged.

The King bore no malice against the Whigs who had once behaved badly but now recognised the danger of revolutionary ideas. To them, the politics of the early 1780s had been something of a game; when their status and property appeared threatened, then they were in deadly earnest. George hinted that he was in favour of men like Lord Auckland joining a coalition with Pitt. Fox was as eager for office as ever and showed some interest in the project, but he insisted on being made Foreign Secretary and demanded that Pitt should give up the premiership. Even Fox's friends admitted that the conditions were impossible. One of the first to desert was the Prince of Wales; exercising his rights as a peer, the Prince went to the House of Lords and publicly dissociated himself from Fox.

It was all very well as a young man to take up elaborate theories to annoy the King, but like the conservative Whigs when faced with the terrible reality of France, the Prince soon made it up with Pitt and his father. Fox was almost alone; men said that he had never discovered the great secret that 'John Bull' was Tory by nature. His supporters in Parliament could have

been accommodated in two hackney carriages. In his isolation, he adopted outright republicanism, but it was not until 1798 that his name was removed from the list of Privy Councillors.

For some time it had seemed likely that England would become involved in war with revolutionary France. Unlike Austria and Prussia, Britain had taken no part in the military intervention which was intended to crush the infant Republic, but Pitt was not very tactful in dealing with the new régime. He must bear some responsibility for the outbreak of war, but even if he had been more diplomatic it is hard to believe that hostilities could have been prevented. So far, Pitt had been a great peace-time Premier; as the example of Lord North suggested, few men were equally successful in both war and peace. At times, Pitt looked as if he was going to follow North; he did not start well as a war leader but he learned from his mistakes and emerged as perhaps the only Premier in British history who has succeeded in both roles.

If anything, the King was even less enthusiastic for war.

The war with Revolutionary France: Pitt is shown as a juggler trying to maintain the stability of England for the King, while a Frenchman wearing the tricolour holds on to his foot.

157

Canaletto's painting of the Thames from
Somerset House, looking towards Westminster Bridge
and the Abbey, executed in about 1750.

JOHN BULL going to the WARS.

John Bull going to the
wars, cartoon by Gillray.

George had enough feeling for a brother monarch to weep
when he heard of Louis XVI's sufferings but, unlike some
sovereigns, he did not go into paroxysms of grief when the
King of France's execution was announced. It is hard to escape
the impression that George regarded the Revolution as divine
punishment for the unnatural support given by the French
monarchy to the American rebels. France declared war on
England and the Netherlands on 1 February 1793; three weeks
later George reviewed three battalions of guards in St James's
Park and went to Greenwich to watch their departure. He
stayed bare-headed on the quay while the ships taking his
soldiers to the Low Countries eased out into the stream.

The war at sea went reasonably well; on land it was disastrous.
The King's friend Admiral Howe won a decisive victory over
the French on 1 June 1794; on 26 June George went down to
Portsmouth to congratulate the Admiral and present him with
a jewelled sword on the flag-ship *Queen Charlotte*. Unfor-

tunately, the British army in the Netherlands, commanded by the Duke of York, put up a poor effort. Frederick's military abilities, parodied in the song 'The Grand Old Duke of York' have been underrated. He improved with experience and was always better than some commanders, but he could not be compared with his French opposite numbers. When a retreat turned into a rout, Pitt was forced to ask the King to recall him. George agreed, although he tried to blame his son's defeats on the cowardice of his Dutch allies.

There were yet more family difficulties for George to face. In April 1793 the Duke of Sussex contracted a secret marriage with Lady Augusta Murray. When the King found out, he obtained a ruling from the ecclesiastical courts that the marriage was void. The marital prospects of the Prince of Wales promised better, but turned out worse. As the Prince of Wales was married to Maria Fitzherbert and in love with Lady Jersey, he was understandably reluctant to make life more complicated. He

In February 1793, George III went to St James's to review battalions of guards before their departure to the Low Countries. This drawing by Rowlandson shows the guards at St James's at the beginning of the nineteenth century.

161

did not want to marry, but he had debts of £650,000 which Parliament would pay only on condition that he took a wife. The Prince agreed but took no interest in the choice; it was George III who decided on Caroline of Brunswick, his own niece and his son's first cousin. The Earl of Malmesbury was sent to Brunswick and reported favourably – perhaps too much so. The couple were married in St James's Palace on 8 April 1795. The Prince had to get himself drunk before he could face the ceremony.

It is hard not to sympathise with the Prince's reaction. His bride was fat and ugly, and dressed in clothes which were garish and vulgar in the extreme. For all his outrageous behaviour, the Prince expected a degree of refinement in women, but Caroline's manners and language would have been more appropriate in a barrack-room than in a palace. She rarely washed and changed her underwear so infrequently that she positively stank. Queen Charlotte saw at once that Caroline would be impossible as a daughter-in-law. The fact that the new Princess of Wales was the daughter of a woman who had deliberately set out to humiliate Charlotte in the early days of her marriage did not make the Queen's feelings any warmer, and she determined to have as little to do with Caroline as possible. George III had not intended to saddle his son with an impossibly unsuitable wife; whatever his private feelings, the fact that he was also choosing a future Queen of England would have prevented him from doing that. For many years he hoped that kindness and persuasion might induce Caroline to behave more decorously. He was to be miserably disappointed. Whatever the King's intentions, with Caroline of Brunswick he more than repaid his son for his lack of filial devotion.

The war had lasted for only two years when there were serious signs of discontent. Some trades were stimulated by government purchases but others suffered from the loss of Continental markets, prices rose but wages did not keep pace, harvests were bad and there was near famine in some parts of the country. While many of the middle classes were doing well, the living standards of the ordinary people deteriorated. The King's popularity declined and the ideas of the French Revolution gained some ground. As George went to open Parliament on 29 October 1795, the state coach was surrounded by people

Caroline of Brunswick, the wife and first cousin of George, Prince of Wales.

shouting 'Bread! Bread! Peace! Peace! No King!' A shot was fired through the window of the state coach as it passed into Old Palace Yard. It was even worse on the way back. Lord Onslow, who was in the coach, declared:

The scene opened and the insulting abuse offered to His Majesty was what I can never think of but with horror, nor ever forget what I felt when they proceeded to throw stones into the coach, several of which hit the King, which he bore with signal patience, but not without sensible marks of indignation and resentment at the indignities offered to his person and office. The glasses were all broken to pieces, and in this situation we were during our passage through the Park. The King took one of the stones out of the cuff of his coat, where it had lodged, and gave it to me saying – 'I make you a

163

Trade in War

The French Revolutionary Wars had a powerful effect upon British trade. As in all times of war, some trades were stimulated by government purchases, but others suffered badly through loss of markets abroad. Moreover, a series of bad harvests sent prices spiralling up, wages remained low, while it was the working classes who suffered most, and were to go on suffering until the cessation of the Napoleonic Wars in 1815.

BELOW Trade card of 1794 for the Dublin and Liverpool packets.

LEFT The Corn Exchange,
a coloured engraving
by Rowlandson.
BELOW Cartoon showing
'The Funeral of Trade'.

present of this, as a mark of the civilities we have met with on our journey today.'

The hostile crowd forced the coach to a halt and the King had to be rescued by the Horse Guards. A few months later, the Queen was hit in the face by a stone as she was leaving Drury Lane Theatre. Although a reward of £1,000 was offered, the man responsible was never caught. It is not surprising that George told Lord Eldon that he would probably be the last King of England. Although George was right to be alarmed, he over-estimated the danger. The people were not yet sufficiently conscious of political issues to pose a serious threat. The French Revolution began as a revolt by a section of the aristocracy supported by the middle classes. In England, apart from a few intellectuals, both groups were fundamentally loyal. When the King went to Covent Garden Theatre on the night of the attack on the state coach, he received a special ovation and the audience demanded that 'God Save the King' should be played three times.

George was a man who could always find comfort in adversity. On 7 January 1796, the Princess of Wales gave birth to a daughter at Carlton House. The baby was christened Charlotte after her grandmother. The King was delighted, but saddened by the complete separation of the girl's parents three months later. Queen Charlotte certainly did not help her daughter-in-law. Following the example of her own mother-in-law, she recruited spies from Caroline's personal servants. Letters from the Princess to her mother, the Duchess of Brunswick, were intercepted and opened by the Queen. Charlotte was not pleased when she discovered that Caroline generally referred to her as 'Old Snuffy', made unkind references to her increasing weight and described in some detail the Queen's taste for gargantuan meals.

The King could still enjoy a pleasant social life. He went to the Eton Montem in 1796 and invited the boys to the terrace at Windsor in the evening. On fine summer nights, George and Charlotte always appeared on the terrace, followed by the family; it must have been a charming sight. On one occasion the Royal Family was delighted to see Fanny Burney who had left her position in the Queen's Household to marry a French émigré, Monsieur d'Arblay. Queen Charlotte went so far as to

An attempt on the King's life in 1795. The execution of Louis XVI had done much to remove the sacred aura surrounding the thrones of Europe, and George was to be prey to several attacks on his life.

depart from her usual rule and allowed her daughters to read Fanny Burney's new novel *Camilla* without first going through the book herself to make sure that it contained nothing improper.

George's good humour was improved by the great naval victories over the Spaniards at Cape St Vincent and over the Dutch at Camperdown. If the French and their allies dominated Europe, at least England had control of the vital sea routes. The King was never an extreme jingoist; he had too much humanity and sense of the bonds linking all European countries to be a rabid nationalist. When the news of Camperdown arrived, Princess Augusta said 'Papa, you are not half happy enough; so many of the Dutch have fallen and so few of our English.'

167

George replied sharply 'Remember Augusta, there are just as many widows and orphans as if they were all English.' The ordinary people were less sensitive. They might not have enough to eat but their patriotism responded to the victories at sea. The King's popularity recovered and the reception he received on his way to the Thanksgiving Service in St Paul's Cathedral was very different from the treatment he had encountered two years earlier.

Although the King was more popular, the execution of the King of France and so many of his Court helped to destroy the semi-divinity which still lingered round the throne. Louis XVI's death had an irresistible fascination for imitative lunatics; some felt they had divine mission, others simply wanted notoriety. On 15 May 1800 George was reviewing the Grenadier Guards in Hyde Park when a man standing close to him was shot in the leg. The affair was dismissed as an accident, but the bullet was probably intended for the King.

That evening George went to the Drury Lane Theatre to see Cibber's comedy *She would and She Would not*. When he entered, the audience stood to cheer and congratulate him on his escape. The King went to the front of the Royal Box and bowed his thanks. Every eye was on George when a man in the pit stood on a bench and fired two pistol shots. The pistol was not a good assassination weapon at this time; it required really exceptional marksmanship to hit one's target at more than a few paces. The distance from the pit to the Royal Box was too far for the assassin to have much chance of success, so that although the man who aimed at the King was a good shot, he was not good enough. The bullets missed by inches and embedded themselves in the panelling at the back of the Box.

At first, George stepped back, but then came forward and looked round through his opera glasses. The Lord Chamberlain, Lord Salisbury, begged him to retire to the ante-room behind the Royal Box where he would be in a less exposed position in the event of another attempt on his life. The King replied 'Sir, you discompose me as well as yourself, I shall not stir one step.' He then ordered the performance to continue and was so calm that he actually went to sleep during the interval. In the meantime, the would-be assassin was seized and taken into the music room beneath the stage. His name was James

s-Hadfield !!!
Attempt on the Life of his Majesty
Theatre on Thursday May 15th 1800

In May 1800, George visited Drury Lane Theatre and was fired at by James Hadfield. The bullets missed the King by inches and were discovered embedded in the Royal Box. James Hadfield was found at his trial to be insane and was committed to Bedlam.

Hadfield, and he had been a soldier in the 15th Light Dragoons. At his trial, it was shown that he had received severe head injuries on active service. A verdict of insanity was returned and he was sent to Bedlam for the rest of his life.

All remarked on the King's calmness and general good health. Despite the anxieties of war, George could take things fairly easily – there were long holidays at Weymouth and voyages in the royal yacht. He was still a hard-working King, but more and more of the day-to-day decisions of government were left to his trusted Minister, Pitt. The result was that the sensitive balance of power between the King and the government seemed to be working in favour of the latter. The royal power which George had reasserted on his accession and triumphantly vindicated in 1784, appeared to be declining as he entered his sixties. Those who believed the process would continue were in for a shock.

Pitt did not want to reduce the power of the Crown; his whole conception of a balanced constitution rebelled against the idea. But the Prime Minister was leading the country in a major European war; it was inevitable that sometimes he would forget the little niceties of consulting the King and simply assume his consent in order to save time. Even in the 1790s there had been clashes between the King and Premier over questions

169

of foreign policy, but then George usually backed down. By 1800, however, the King decided that Pitt had gone too far and determined to redress the balance in his own favour.

George was especially interested in questions concerning the Church. He did not take Queen Elizabeth's doctrine that as Supreme Governor of the Church of England, the Sovereign had no need to consult Parliament on religious matters. He did believe, however, that he should have greater freedom of action in ecclesiastical affairs than in ordinary secular questions. George had no intention of allowing Pitt to dictate to him on this subject. If it came to a choice between a Minister supported by a majority in Parliament and George's idea of his duty to God, there was no doubt that he would choose God.

The King was an admirer of Dr Stuart, the Bishop of St David's, and hoped to promote him to a more important position. In July 1800 the primacy of the Anglican Church in Ireland became vacant and the King suggested that the government should make Stuart Archbishop of Armagh. Pitt and his colleagues were ready to accept Stuart, but they offered him the appointment on condition that he took a smaller salary than his predecessor. George was furious and successfully demanded that the government withdraw its impertinent conditions.

More serious trouble was coming. Pitt the Younger was not the first or the last English statesman whose career has been ruined by an essentially Irish issue. The eighteenth century was a time of relative calm in Ireland and the country enjoyed a degree of autonomy. A separate Parliament met in Dublin; although the assembly, Gratton's Parliament, was even more corrupt than its English counterpart and only Protestants were members, after a fashion it did represent Irish interests. The ideas of the French Revolution gained considerable support in Ireland; there were both Catholics and Protestants who took up the cause of Irish nationalism. In 1798 a rebellion broke out which received support from France.

Pitt was anxious to close a dangerous loop-hole. He decided to abolish the Dublin Parliament and introduce Irish members to Westminster. The idea had the added attraction that the patronage resources of Ireland would now be controlled by the British government and would help to compensate for the reductions made by the recent reforms. The King gave the Act

170

of Union his enthusiastic support. The Prime Minister, however, regarded the Union as only the first stage in a general settlement of the Irish problem. In the face of the French threat, he wanted to make sure of the loyalty of a group who were discriminated against under the existing system. Roman Catholics who possessed the necessary property were allowed to vote, but they were effectively excluded from Parliament by legislation which required new members to take oaths which specifically repudiated the central tenets of the Roman Catholic faith. Pitt wanted to make the Irish members at Westminster more representative of their constituents. He promised a number of leading Roman Catholics, including members of the Irish hierarchy, that in return for their support for the Act of Union, he would bring in a bill to enable Roman Catholics to sit in Parliament without repudiating their faith.

The Act of Union on its own was unfair to Ireland, but there was much to be said for Pitt's package deal as a whole. It would

In 1799, Pitt decided to abolish Gratton's Parliament in Dublin and to introduce Irish members at Westminster. This cartoon by Cruikshank compares the Union with Ireland to that with Scotland, made a century earlier. Henry Dundas, the supreme political 'operator' north of the border, reads from a folio History of Scotland, while Pitt joins the reluctant hands of Paddy and John Bull.

be too much to say that, had it been implemented, Ireland would have been saved from all its future misery; its failure, however, certainly made most of the later troubles inevitable. The King was largely responsible for the defeat of Catholic Emancipation. It was a measure favoured by most of the leading politicians, but its postponement for almost thirty years is a striking demonstration of the continuing power of the Crown.

Pitt did not handle the King well and deliberately kept him in the dark. George only heard about the Catholic Relief Bill on 28 February 1801, four days before the measure was due to be announced in Parliament. He was astounded and, repeating the tactic he had used to defeat Fox's India Bill, said that he would regard anyone who voted for the Bill as his personal enemy. To modern eyes, George's position is hard to appreciate, but there was some justification for it. He certainly did not wish to persecute Catholics, but he believed that in time of war it was foolish to raise such an explosive issue. Even discussion of the subject would raise expectations on the Catholic side which were bound to be disappointed and, at the same time, create a sense of fear amongst Protestants which could well lead to violence. George was a good deal more perceptive than the politicians in his recognition of the sad truth that Irish issues can rarely be settled 'rationally'.

The King considered Pitt's measure 'Jacobinical' but, above all, he was convinced that if he accepted the Prime Minister's proposals, he would be guilty of blasphemy in breaking his coronation oath. At his coronation, the Archbishop had asked George:

> Will you to the utmost of your power maintain the laws of God, the true profession of the Gospel and the Protestant reformed religion established by law? And will you preserve unto the bishops and clergy of this realm, and the churches committed to their charge, all such rights and privileges as by law do or shall appertain unto them or any of them?

The King had replied 'All this I promise to do', and as far as he was concerned, that settled the matter; he was very impatient of the clever people Pitt sent to St James's Palace to persuade him that acceptance of Catholic Emancipation would not mean a violation of the coronation oath. He believed that the moment he agreed to the measure he would cease to be King of England in the sight of God. At the back of his mind, George had a bad conscience about the House of Stuart. He had persuaded himself that the House of Hanover had become the legitimate line because of its solemn undertaking to defend the Protestant religion. If he conceded Catholic Emancipation, there would be no difference between the claims of the House of Hanover and the House of Stuart. George never believed Protestant propaganda that the Old Pretender had been a foundling introduced to Mary of Modena's bed in a warming pan. If the King betrayed the reformed religion, the throne would rightly belong to the elder and more direct line. Now that the Young Pretender was dead and his brother Henry a Cardinal, Charles Emmanuel II of Savoy – a descendant of Charles I's daughter, Henrietta, and Philip of Orléans – would be the true king of England. Rather than so disgrace himself, many people believed that George would be ready to go to the block.

It is easy to appreciate Pitt's horror at the King's somewhat hysterical reaction to a measure which, as a rational man, the Prime Minister believed essential for the security and long-term stability of the United Kingdom. As the events of 1784 had demonstrated, no politician stood a chance when faced with a combination of royal power and hostile public opinion. The King would always succeed when he had the country behind him. The educated élite might favour Catholic Emancipation but Protestant prejudices were still very strong amongst the ordinary people. There can be no doubt that Pitt's measure would have been extremely unpopular and would have almost certainly produced serious rioting. Within the establishment, the King was supported by the Lord Chancellor, the Royal Family, most judges and the clergy of the Anglican Church almost to a man.

Pitt knew when he was beaten. It is said that he behaved well by going quietly but, in reality, he had little choice. The Prime Minister said that he would resign unless the King accepted the Catholic Relief Bill. George did not take kindly to an ultimatum, even from someone who had served him faithfully for seventeen years. He said he would be sorry to lose Pitt and, as a special favour, he was prepared to overlook the Prime Minister's recent behaviour. If Pitt would drop his plans, the King would

OVERLEAF The House of Commons at Westminster in 1793, painted by Karl Anton Hickel.

173

OPPOSITE ABOVE
'The Constant Couple',
Farmer George and his
wife riding from St James's
to Windsor; cartoon
of 1786.
BELOW The re-electing of
Reynard (C. J. Fox) in
1783. Fox is being carried
in triumph by the geese
who mistakenly believe
him to be the Man of
the People.

allow him to continue in office; otherwise, the resignation would be accepted. The Prime Minister felt that his promise to the Roman Catholics prevented him from compromising. He was succeeded by the Speaker, Henry Addington. It was less than a week since George had heard of the plan; in the face of royal displeasure, Parliamentary majorities, oratorical brilliance and wizardry with figures availed very little. After almost a generation sheltering behind Pitt, George emerged into an exposed position in politics and prepared to take on all-comers.

The Catholic Emancipation issue and Pitt's resignations caused George much distress. He complained of lack of sleep and this may have been the trigger for another bout of the terrible illness of 1788, although on this occasion the attack was less severe. The same symptoms of biliousness, constipation, muscular pains, the appearance of a cold, hoarseness, dark urine, fever and a racing pulse gradually asserted themselves. George put the blame squarely on Pitt. The crucial question was whether the disease would progress to its extreme forms of insanity and coma. The Rev. Thomas Willis, son of Francis Willis, called at Buckingham House on 16 February 1801 but saw no sign of disturbance. During the next few days, the King's manner became more hurried but he presided as usual at a Privy Council on 20 February. George was collected on some subjects but confused on others; Pitt said 'His Majesty's mind is not in its proper state'. That was not the same as declaring that the King was mad. Addington, the new Prime Minister, suggested that George should adopt the old folk remedy of sleeping on a pillow filled with dried hops to cure his insomnia. At least that did no harm.

On 22 February Addington and the Duke of York sent for Francis Willis's son John. With the memory of his earlier torments, George was understandably reluctant to see Willis and tried to slip out of the room. He was cornered and told sharply that he must stay in his apartments. Willis sent for four strong men to act as the King's keepers, forbade him to see members of his family and reserved the right to exclude the highest officers of State – all this when George's behaviour could still be attributed to fever. The descriptions of his conduct do not accord with any usual definition of insanity, nor was there any hint of violence.

The Constant Couple

The Re-Electing of Reynard,
or Fox the Pride of the Geese

John Willis and his brother Thomas were in absolute control. Francis Willis was now an old man, and declined an invitation to attend the King. When the Lord Chancellor called with documents requiring the King's signature he was denied access to the sick room. The papers were signed with only Thomas Willis as a witness, an entirely illegal procedure. Thomas Willis exploited his situation as an intermediary between the government and the King to such an extent that, according to George Rose, he was the real executive authority for a fortnight.

The situation was complicated by Addington's strange position. The former Speaker was generally regarded as *locum tenens* for Pitt until some compromise could be arranged over Catholic Emancipation. While the outgoing Ministers had resigned, they could not give up their seals of office because of George's illness. As they held the seals, they were the only people entitled to transact government business. Either there were two governments or none. In fact, there was surprisingly little difficulty. The Regency Bill of 1789 was to hand and all parties agreed to avoid the unpleasant business of discussing the King's illness in Parliament. Pitt and Addington got on fairly well and the Prince of Wales was now too frightened of revolution to ask for help from his old friends, the Foxite Whigs. On a personal level, the Prince's behaviour was no better than in 1788. He exaggerated his father's illness and gaily told the former French Premier, Calonne, that the King was '*plus fou que jamais*'.

George slipped into a coma for a day but emerged on 24 February. He was confused and, according to John Willis, could not recognise any letter of the alphabet. Gradually he improved, but the heavy doses of James's powder, calomel and tartar emetic had weakened him. At sixty-three, he could not recover so completely as he had twelve years earlier. His vision was distorted and he had a tendency to cry at anything – a sign that there had probably been some brain damage.

The damage cannot have been serious. The King was well enough to receive the seals from Pitt on 14 March and preside at a Privy Council three days later. It was a peculiar situation. Although George was thought well enough to resume his role as Sovereign, he was still treated as if he were mad. As he grew stronger, he became increasingly impatient at the continued

'I wish to God I might die for I am going to be mad'

restraint. The Queen trusted the Willises but did not want to antagonise her husband. She wavered between wanting them to go and urging them to stay to see that there would be no relapse. Whilst Pitt would have dealt firmly with recalcitrant doctors, the new government was still feeling its way. Thomas Willis actually received Cabinet papers about negotiations for a peace treaty with France. Once he had tasted power, he was reluctant to give it up. He declared that the patient was quite well enough to dispense with his other doctors, but it was essential to retain his own services.

When the King arranged a Drawing Room for 25 March, Willis put blisters on his legs and administered emetics so that he could not attend. To say that such conduct was unprofessional is to put it mildly. George had had enough – on 30 March 1801 he told Willis to go.

Although the order came from the King, of whose sanity there could be no question, Willis did not intend to obey. He argued that George must be mad because he disliked the Willis family! Willis disappeared for a few days and on 18 April the King was able to ride out to Blackheath to see his only grand-child, Princess Charlotte. Despite evidence of recovery, Willis persuaded the Queen and her daughters that they would not be safe alone with the King. Princess Elizabeth obligingly wrote to Thomas Willis asking him to return.

The problem was 'how to take His Majesty into our power' without his consent. Neither the Queen nor Addington was eager to give an order which might bring them a great deal of trouble. They certainly had no authority to do so; the King's 'insanity' had not been mentioned in Parliament and, legally, he retained all the powers of a monarch. Eventually, Charlotte was pressed into authorising her husband's kidnap.

Thomas Willis hoped to catch George in London; to his dis-comfort, he saw the King riding up the Mall on his way to Kew. There was no alternative but to give chase. The supposedly insane monarch was a better horseman than his medical adviser and reached Kew well in advance of his pursuers. At seven next morning, Thomas Willis, his brother John and six assistants gathered outside the house. Again, George gave them the slip by going out of a back door; perhaps he was rather foolish to go to the house occupied by the Prince of Wales.

Strawberry Hill Gothick

In 1747 Horace Walpole bought a modest house by the Thames and began to reconstruct it as 'a little Gothick Castle'. He produced an imaginative edifice, rather than a studied reproduction of a Gothic building as previous revivalists had attempted to do. Thus the style known as Strawberry Hill Gothick came into being.

George III was brought up in the Classical taste by Sir William Chambers and maintained a conservative attitude towards architecture until Chambers' death. Thereafter he became attracted to Gothic ideas and at the turn of the century he commissioned James Wyatt to produce a great baronial castle in medieval style at Kew. LEFT The Strawberry Room at Lee Priory, designed in the Gothick style by James Wyatt, between 1782 and 1790.

While the King was taking breakfast, Willis burst in and
began to speak of 'the necessity there is that your Majesty
should be immediately under control again'. George turned
very pale and said 'Sir, I will never forgive you.' It was not an
unreasonable attitude. The King tried to escape but he was out-
numbered eight to one. He was taken back to Kew House and
kept as a prisoner for a whole month. He was not allowed to see
members of his family, who lived two hundred yards away, and
was kept low by heavy doses of emetics and by bleeding. All the
time, he was writing perfectly sensible and lucid letters to
members of the government. By all the laws of the land it was
high treason.

The King could not be mad and sane at the same time. There
was only one way of getting rid of Thomas Willis. The new
Lord Chancellor, Lord Eldon, managed to break the cordon
and George told him that unless he was given his freedom, he
would refuse to sign any government papers. Eldon supported
him and together they walked out of the house. There was
nothing Willis could do. By the end of June George was well
enough to go to Weymouth. It was suggested that Dr John
Willis should accompany the royal party. The King soon
quashed that. In the end the Willis brothers had to be bought
off; Dr John received £5,000, Dr Robert £3,000 and Rev.
Thomas £2,000. Lady Anne Hamilton made many wild and
extravagant claims but, for once, she was guilty of understate-
ment when she declared 'His Majesty's disorder did not require
that close and solitary confinement so arbitrarily imposed upon
him.' Altogether it was one of the most disgraceful episodes in
the history of royal medicine.

8 The Last Years
1801-20

IT IS EASY TO UNDERSTAND that the Queen might be taken in by a man who was supposed to have 'cured' her husband in the past, but the Prime Minister's role seems more sinister. Addington, or rather his relations, had changed his mind about returning power to Pitt at the earliest opportunity. He now saw no reason why he should not stay in office for some years. The cause of the friction between the King and the ex-Premier had disappeared. Pitt was upset by allegations that he had caused George's illness and was told by Thomas Willis that an undertaking from him not to raise the Catholic Emancipation issue again was essential to preserve the King's life. Pitt agreed and the news cheered George enormously. Even in his illness, the King felt sufficient regard for Pitt to make an anonymous offer to pay his debts. If Pitt had had free access to George whilst the Addington administration was still very feeble, there was a possibility that he would have returned to power in a few weeks. Such a development was not very likely, but it is easy to understand why the new Prime Minister should have wished to prevent his master seeing too much of the outside world. Thomas Willis, who thought Pitt was destined to eternal damnation for even contemplating the admission of Roman Catholics to Parliament, was happy to collaborate. Addington's questionable conduct went unpunished. George did not discover the 'understanding' with Willis and felt grateful to the former Speaker for coming to his aid when Pitt had been urging him to commit a terrible sin. At the end of his illness, the King pressed the Prime Minister to accept White Lodge in Richmond Park and personally supervised improvements.

Once freed from Willis, George's health improved rapidly. He visited Cuffnells at the edge of the New Forest and then went on to Weymouth. He wrote to Richard Hurd, the Bishop of Worcester, that the sea-bathing had done him much good. When Lord Malmesbury saw the King in November 1801, he had the impression of a man who was beginning to show his age, but not much more so than most people in their mid-sixties. He stooped a little more and was rather less firm on his legs but his conversation was entirely sensible.

Unfortunately, the holiday was brief and the King had to return to London to face the serious question of peace with France. The peace was very popular in the country but its terms were disadvantageous to Britain. France kept all her conquests while Britain gave up hers, with the exception of Trinidad, and received no commercial advantages for her sacrifice. Sir Philip Francis said 'It is a peace which everybody is glad of though nobody is proud of.' Fox and Addington were delighted but many doubted whether the peace would last. The King was right in describing the treaty of Amiens as 'an experimental peace'. Although Addington gained some popularity by abolishing income tax, George was reluctant to sanction any corresponding reduction in the size of the armed services.

Less than a year passed before new French aggression confirmed the King's reservations. War seemed inevitable. Pitt was not the great war leader his father had been, but he was much better than Addington and a number of influential men were calling for his return. By March 1803 even members of the Cabinet were begging the King to dismiss their chief and recall Pitt. Pitt himself was disgusted by the clear evidence of Addington's incompetence. On 20 March 1803 he rejected an offer of subordinate office in the Cabinet. Like his father in a similar situation, Pitt would return as Prime Minister or not at all. Unlike Chatham, however, he was careful to add 'the change must be by the King's desire'. The position George had fought for throughout his reign was expressed in these eight words. Pitt's deference reflected the national mood. Devotion to the Crown was increased by the revelation of yet another conspiracy, this time by a half-crazed colonel, Edward Despard. Despard planned to kill the King by firing a piece of cannon – recently captured from the French and then on display in St James's Park – at the state coach on its way to Parliament. Despite evidence of Despard's gallantry from Lord Nelson, the Colonel and six of his supporters were hanged from a gibbet on the roof of Horsemonger Lane Gaol.

The very fact of the negotiations between Pitt and Addington was an indication that the delicate balance of power was again moving away from the Crown. The discussions were based on an assumption that the participants could settle who was to be next Prime Minister without reference to the King. George was furious. Addington was really most to blame; as Prime Minister, the responsibility to inform the King of what was going on clearly rested with him. Pitt repeatedly asked to be told of the

'A peace which everybody is glad of though nobody is proud of'

Invasion cartoon by Gillray showing George III and Queen Charlotte watching the advance of Napoleon.

Published Feb.ʸ 10ᵗʰ 1804 by H. Humphrey
St James's Street. London.

The KING of BROBDINGNAG and

'I often used to Row for my own diversion, as well as that of the Q—
and shew my art by steering starboard & larboard; — However, r
those about him could not make them contain. — This made me
out of all degree of equality or comparison with him.

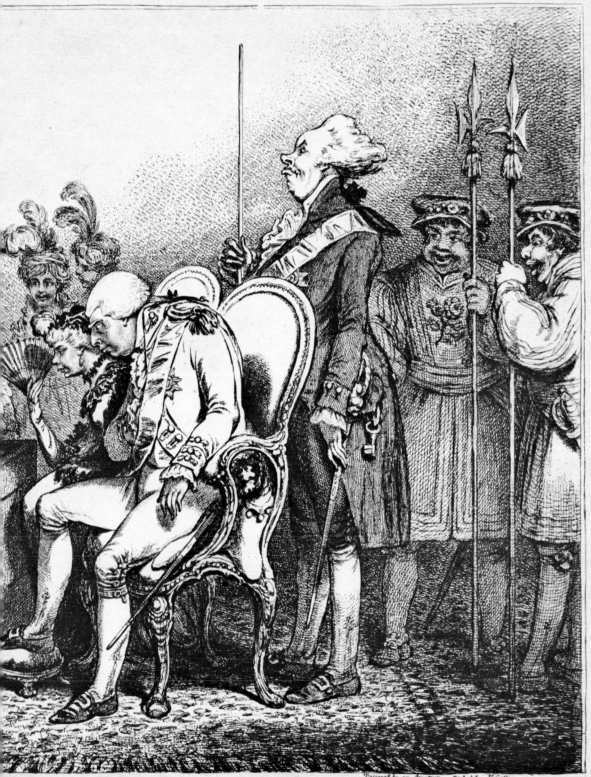

Designed by an Amateur :— Etched by J. Gillray

ER . (Plate 2.ᵈ) ___ Scene."Gulliver manœuvring with his little Boat in the Cistern". Vide . Swifts Gulliver

..ies, who thought themselves well entertained with my skill & agility. Sometimes I would put up my Sail
..oduced nothing else besides a loud laughter, which all the respect due to his Majesty from
..ain an attempt it is for a man to endeavour to do himself honour among those, who are
..ge to Brobdingnag

English Furniture *of the eighteenth century*

RIGHT Design by Thomas
Sheraton for a library table
with folding book and
music rests, 1792.
BELOW Thomas
Chippendale's design for a
commode and candle
stands, 1761.

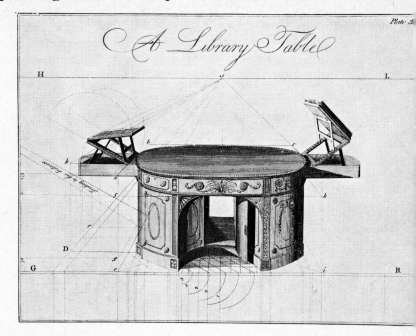

A Library Table

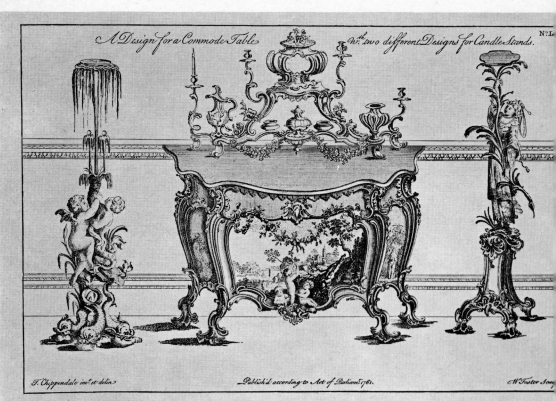

A Design for a Commode Table   *w.th two different Designs for Candle Stands.*

RIGHT Mahogany
sideboard dating from the
1770s.
BELOW LEFT Chair of
the second quarter of
the century.
BELOW RIGHT Mahogany
armchair of *c.* 1760.

King's views; it would have been improper for him to approach the Sovereign directly. Addington misrepresented Pitt's conduct and persuaded his master that it was he who sought to undermine the royal prerogative.

George came to believe that Pitt had a plan for 'putting the Crown into a Commission'. If he really thought that, then there is no doubt that his judgment was deteriorating. The decline should not be exaggerated and the King's comment when the negotiations broke down 'It is a foolish business from one end to the other; it was begun ill, conducted ill and terminated ill' was not far wrong.

There were debates in Parliament on the desirability of peace or war with France, but the disputes ended when the French attacked Hanover. The King's forces surrendered to General Mortier on 3 June 1803. George always expressed love of Hanover but he never went there and bore its loss stoically. There were now signs that the French were preparing to invade England. Napoleon recognised the difficulties of transporting an army to England whilst the Channel was dominated by the Royal Navy, but he felt that the invasion was needed to crush French opposition to his régime. Britain united in its determination to resist and patriotism focussed on the King. In the event of invasion there would have been some collaborators, probably rather more than was likely in 1940, but still their numbers would not have been large. On 26 October 1803 George reviewed the Volunteer Corps of the City of London, over twelve thousand men. At the entrance to Hyde Park he got out of his carriage and mounted a charger. He was attended by his seven sons on horseback and accompanied by some of the exiled Bourbon princes. The crowd, estimated at two hundred thousand, cheered wildly. Lord Eldon said it was the finest sight he had ever witnessed. Altogether, forty-six thousand men from the London area joined the Volunteers.

George intended to lead his troops into battle if the French invaded. Although he was convinced that any such invasion would fail, provisional arrangements were made to transfer the Queen, her daughters, the Crown Jewels and important papers to Worcester. The King may not have had much military experience but his plans to concentrate forces inland in Kent and Essex and then strike wherever his enemy made a beachhead –

ATTENTION

An Upright Position, the muzzle of the Piece placed in the Interval of the right Shoulder. Right hand extended down the Sling. Left hand straight down the thigh.

Rowlandson's drawing of
a Westminster Volunteer.

rather than string his forces out along the coast – seems eminently sensible. Even the Prince of Wales, a corpulent voluptuary of forty, was loud in demanding active military employment. Despite the Prince's claims to have made a special study of the art of war, the request was rejected. Although the Royal Family displayed admirable patriotism, the services of greater minds than theirs were called for if the country was about to receive the personal attention of Napoleon Bonaparte.

In February 1804 the King had another attack of his old complaint, with symptoms following in their now familiar way. It is doubtful whether the King's mind was deranged at all in 1804 but he was growing old and the attack gave him more physical pain than its earlier visitations. Armed with an authority from

The north terrace at Windsor Castle: painting by Sandby.

Addington, the Willis brothers presented themselves at Buckingham House on the morning of 13 February 1804. When they tried to see the King, their way was blocked by the Dukes of Kent and Cumberland. The Prime Minister appeared and was told by the Duke of Kent that he had promised the King that if the illness returned, no one connected with the Willis family would be allowed near him. At last, it seemed, the Royal Family were showing some sense.

The King's sons had been inconsiderate enough in the past; filial devotion may have come with greater maturity, but there may be another explanation. 'Restraint' was probably less attractive to anyone who feared that there was even a possibility of being subjected to the same treatment themselves. Dr Zimmermann, the German medical man who attended the Dukes of York and Sussex when they were ill in Hanover, had

192

already suggested that their disease was caused by hereditary factors. After 1803 the Duke of Kent suffered badly from 'biliousness'; the appearance of a symptom which always manifested itself at the beginning of the King's attacks may explain both the Duke's promise and his determination not to admit Thomas Willis.

The Prime Minister, who was not likely to be influenced by such considerations, still believed in Willis. He turned for support to the King's regular doctors only to be told by William Heberden that a renewal of 'restraint' would probably kill the patient. Addington was forced to drop Willis, but he produced another 'mad' doctor, Dr Simmons, whose methods differed little from those of George's old tormentors. Despite Simmons's attempts to keep the King in a strait jacket more or less permanently, George was only ill for a fortnight.

Much of the credit for the recovery must go to the Lord Chancellor. As a politician, Eldon was reactionary by any standards; as a lawyer, his management of the court of Chancery is open to serious criticism; but, as a man, George could not have had a better or a more humane friend. Those who encountered Eldon in court knew to their cost that he was not a man who could be brow-beaten. He had seen enough of Willis's methods to have a low opinion of them and possessed the arrogance needed to put doctors firmly in their place. When Simmons persuaded the Queen that it was unsafe even to see the King, Eldon called at Buckingham House and insisted on taking George for a walk in the gardens. The King seemed excited and occasionally tearful, but the Chancellor was adamant that his conversation was completely lucid. Eldon pressed the doctors to admit that the King was fit enough to transact government business and then pointed to the absurdity of keeping such a person in a strait jacket.

When he was better, George tried to give Eldon a watch and chain he had worn himself for the previous twenty years, but the Chancellor declined on the grounds that the gift would increase the complaints of those who already resented the King's friendship with him. George accepted the refusal, but then burst into tears. A few months later, when Eldon was sitting in Chancery, a court messenger placed a red box in front of him. The box contained the King's watch which had been cleaned and repaired and a note saying that at least illness enabled one to distinguish real from pretended friends. One Victorian writer, Heneage Jesse, actually claimed that the gift indicated that George's mind was 'still in an enfeebled state'. It is hard to see the logic of this assertion. Eldon fully deserved this special mark of royal favour; by his firmness with the King's doctors, he was certainly responsible for prolonging his active life.

The Addington ministry was obviously incapable of going on much longer. While still convalescent the King showed himself capable of decisive action. The government was defeated on 25 April 1804 and resigned four days later. George feared a Pitt-Fox coalition and was hurt by Pitt's repeated refusal of invitations to Buckingham House and Kew. It did not take him long to realise that Pitt would never wittingly endanger the prerogative. Pitt considered offering Fox a place, but when the King made it clear that Fox was unacceptable, he was prepared to accept the royal veto.

On Monday 7 May 1804 Eldon breakfasted with Pitt. The former Premier had been forced to leave his house in St James's Street and was living in reduced circumstances off Baker Street. Eldon took him to see the King at Buckingham House. Pitt congratulated George on looking better than after his illness in 1801. The King replied kindly 'It is not to be wondered at: I was then on the point of parting with an old friend, and I am now about to regain one.' George agreed to everything Pitt proposed except Fox's accession to the Cabinet, although he would agree to any position which did not involve personal contact with his old enemy.

Whatever the constitutional issues, George was probably right in seeking to prevent a coalition government which he realised was unlikely to last long. Fox himself accepted the exclusion with good grace and said that he did not wish to prevent any of his supporters taking office under Pitt. The opposition leaders met at Carlton House, the London home of the Prince of Wales, and decided to decline any offers. The new Prime Minister was gazetted on 12 May 1804 and retained about half his predecessor's Cabinet.

The opposition meeting at Carlton House was a sign that the Prince of Wales was resuming his contacts with the Whig party.

OPPOSITE John Scott, 1st Earl of Eldon: portrait by Thomas Lawrence.

Although the Regency Bill had been prepared, it had never been implemented and the Prince had never enjoyed more authority than any other subject. He was becoming impatient at his father's longevity. Whatever the Prince of Wales might do, the King had always been able to rely on his wife's good intentions. Now he had reason to doubt even this. Despite her good qualities, Queen Charlotte developed an unreasoning, superstitious revulsion towards any form of mental illness. She became too ready to take any sign of independence in her husband as the prelude to another attack. George was certainly restless and dismissed pages and grooms of the Bedchamber who had been around him during his illness. The action may have been ungrateful, but the desire to be rid of those who had witnessed his recent humiliations is very understandable. The Duke of Kent noted 'a great coolness towards our mother'. The Prince of Wales was quickly reconciled with the Queen and, supported by most of the Royal Family, he accused the new government of hiding the real extent of his father's illness in order to deny him the Regency.

Eldon was able to evade the Prince's demands for a few weeks and then produce his master, clearly in full possession of his faculties, at the opening of Parliament on 31 July 1804. Despite conclusive evidence of the King's sanity, the Prince persisted in regarding his father with the arrogant contempt usually adopted to the mentally ill. The Prince had arranged to meet the King at Kew and then haughtily ordered Eldon to inform George that he had changed his mind and would not be going. The Chancellor would not tolerate such conduct from anyone. Whatever George's condition, he was entitled to the respect due to an anointed King. Quite properly, the Chancellor refused to take such an insulting message. He replied 'I am his Majesty's Chancellor, and it is for me to judge what messages I ought to take to his Majesty.'

George got rid of Simmons on 20 August 1804, and four days later, he set out for Weymouth. The illness had made him an old man and, instead of going into the sea, he was forced to confine himself to baths of tepid sea water. Even so, the journey gives proof that, at sixty-six, George still had plenty of strength and endurance. After dining at the Star and Garter Inn at Andover, he travelled through the night to Weymouth and arrived at five in the morning. Two hours later, he was walking on the Esplanade and, after breakfasting, he mounted his horse to review the Hanoverian Legion. In the afternoon he inspected the German Legion, the Somerset Militia and the Weymouth Volunteers. He addressed the foreign soldiers in perfect German, talked about ships to sailors and agriculture to Dorset farmers. For a man supposedly convalescent, it was an exacting programme. On 8 September there was a splendid ball to celebrate the King's forty-second wedding anniversary, on 22 September a review of the fleet followed by another ball at which the King remained till after midnight, and on 29 September a party on board the royal yachts. When the Court was staying at Cuffnells, Princess Amelia was thrown from her horse. Amelia behaved with considerable courage and the King observed 'I thank heaven there is but one of my children who wants courage; and I will not name *him* because he is to succeed me.'

'I thank heaven there but is one of my children who wants courage'

George must have been grieved by the increasing evidence of hostility in his wife. The King's most sympathetic doctor, William Heberden, was annoyed that the Queen always put the worst possible construction on the King's behaviour. Charlotte now refused to allow George to sleep in her bed and insisted that at least two German ladies-in-waiting should remain with her all night. As he grew older, George lost some of the German traits which caused him so much difficulty in the early years of his reign. In the last years, Charlotte seemed to revert to her original nationality and surrounded herself with Germans almost to the exclusion of English company. After forty years of generally happy marriage, the couple had less and less in common. George particularly resented his wife's coldness to their only grandchild. It is sad that the last years should have been clouded in this way; perhaps there were faults on both sides, but few people can have taken the King's threat to find a mistress very seriously. On the other hand, William Heberden was adamant that after 1804 Charlotte showed a manifest distaste for her husband. He could not understand why; the Queen was well beyond the age when menopausal difficulties could have explained her conduct. At one time Charlotte had been popular, but now she was a fat, ugly and unpleasant old woman. She had considerable ability and is alleged to have made nearly £400,000 from speculations on the Stock Exchange. At her

197

death, her private possessions filled twenty-nine large carts. In fact the Queen's avarice and meanness – she delayed payment to her daughters' tutors for as long as fifteen years – became notorious and certainly did not add to the prestige of the Crown.

In one sense, George's recovery was incomplete. Attacks of porphyria can damage the eyes, and in some unknown way, the disease appears to encourage the growth of cataracts. After George's visit to Weymouth it was reported that he had nearly lost the sight of his right eye and that, even with the strongest spectacles, he had difficulty in reading by candlelight. In the summer of 1805 the left eye was affected. An operation for cataracts, known as 'couching' was sometimes undertaken in the early nineteenth century. Without anaesthetics, the operation was excruciatingly painful and was not often successful, although it did work on George's son, the Duke of Sussex, in 1835. In the King's case, the operation was never attempted.

Until the age of sixty-eight, the King conducted an enormous correspondence with little secretarial assistance. Now Colonel Herbert Taylor, formerly secretary to the Duke of York, was employed to read despatches and take dictation. After an attack of inflammation, the King was encouraged by his oculist, Sir Jonathan Wathen Waller, to hope that the irritation would disperse his cataract. George actually thought there was a little improvement but his hopes were disappointed. The King's small precise handwriting degenerated into a large scrawl which covered a page in about five lines. His last attempts to write in 1809 show that he could not even see when the ink in his pen had run out.

Not even the approach of blindness could prevent the King from playing an active role in politics. There was so little affection within the Royal Family that relations between its members were a matter of politics pure and simple. George had long given up any hope of a meaningful reconciliation with his eldest son, but he was determined to see that his granddaughter Princess Charlotte, who was expected to be Queen one day, should be properly brought up. The King had good reason for thinking that Carlton House was not a suitable place for a young girl, while the Princess's mother, though deserving sympathy for the treatment she received from her husband, was really a

OPPOSITE Princess Amelia, George III's favourite daughter, who died in 1810: portrait by Sir William Beechey.

silly and indiscreet woman. Princess Charlotte was a charming girl who soon became a great favourite with her grandfather. At first the Prince of Wales agreed to entrust his daughter's education to the King. Before leaving for Weymouth, George had made arrangements for the Princess to come to live at Windsor Castle. During the King's holiday, Lady Melbourne and Mrs Fox persuaded Charlotte's father to change his mind. When the King returned, his son first denied that he had ever agreed to give up his daughter and then claimed that his father's insanity absolved him from his promise. Eventually, the King got his way and took great pains in supervising his grand-daughter's education.

Unlike his predecessor, Pitt always consulted the King before undertaking any political initiative. In December 1804 George was delighted when the Premier suggested that Addington should join the government. Addington took office as Lord President of the Council and was created Viscount Sidmouth. During negotiations, George invited Addington to dine *en tête à tête*. No politician since Bute had been given such an honour. The King's taste for simple food remained unaltered; the meal consisted of mutton chops, followed by steamed pudding.

George was being rather astute in maximising good will at a time when a serious disagreement with Pitt was in the offing. Dr John Moore, the Archbishop of Canterbury, died on 18 January 1805 after a long illness. Pitt was anxious to promote his old Cambridge tutor, Dr Tomline, now Bishop of Lincoln. The King was determined to appoint his friend Dr Manners Sutton, the Dean of Windsor. George objected to Tomline as too much of a party man; as soon as he heard of Moore's death, he hurried to the Deanery and arrived during dinner. Sutton left the table and met his visitor in a small dressing room. The King took his hand and said 'My Lord Archbishop of Canterbury, I wish you joy. Not a word; go back to your guests.' When Pitt arrived next morning, he began to praise Tomline's merits but he was cut short and bluntly informed of Sutton's appointment. The Prime Minister was angry but there was nothing he could do. Once again the royal prerogative had triumphed. The real decline in royal influence dates from the Regency and the reign of George IV, who was too lazy to attend to business.

The success put George into a good humour. There was more

social life at Windsor Castle than for many years. On 25 February the King gave a splendid ball for his younger daughters and on 23 April, St George's Day, new Knights of the Garter were installed with all the traditional splendour. George caused surprise by wearing an enormous curled wig of the kind favoured by Charles II. Wigs had been getting smaller, at least for men, throughout the eighteenth century and younger men ceased to wear them at all in the 1790s. Even on ceremonial occasions, only small wigs were worn; George's was so vast that it almost covered his face and reached to his chest. Otherwise, the King behaved entirely normally. It was rumoured in Windsor that George had worn the wig to annoy the Queen. Although the occasion was perhaps not the best to display a sense of humour, eccentric dress is no proof of insanity.

Although the King could hardly recognise anyone more than three yards away, he was determined to live as normally as possible. His letters, though difficult to read and fewer in numbers, were entirely lucid. He still rode a horse and often visited the cottages of his estate workers. On occasion, and at some danger to himself, he went out with the Royal Stag Hounds. A proposed royal tour of the Midlands in the summer of 1805 had to be cancelled but Lord Henley's description of the King on 1 November hardly suggests senility:

'Our good King continues, mind and body, sight excepted, better than I have seen him for years'

> Our good King continues, mind and body, sight excepted, better than I have seen him for years. I forgot to tell you that he plays at Commerce without any further assistance than he derives from his spectacles. He was last night in good spirits. This morning I met him in the Park, at ten o'clock and rode with him till quarter past one. He was cheerful, and we had more than one of his hearty laughs, which I have not heard for some time. He talked to me, indeed in an affecting manner, of his situation, saying that he had tried this morning but in vain, to read the docket of one of his despatches. Lady Henley says that he presented the muffins to the ladies last night in his old jocose and good humoured manner.

Many of the King's own generation were predeceasing him. His last surviving brother, the Duke of Gloucester, died on 25 August 1805. Others were much younger. George was grieved by the death of the national hero, Lord Nelson, at the Battle of Trafalgar on 21 October 1805, but the greatest blow was the

Within the image (speech bubbles and caption, part of the cartoon):

"We'll teach you, you French Frog eaters what it is to board on English man of War, how you forgot the Battle of the Nile already"

"D——mme Jack, why here we have got both Parlezvous & Dons at the same time, upon us"

"what you'll never do so again eh, I'll just take off a Wing or two by way of Security"

AN ENGLISH SET-TOO, or British Tars clearing the Deck of the Temeraire of French and Spain

a Circumstance which occur'd during the Battle of Trafalgar 21 Oct 1805 which strongly marks the invincible spirit of British Seamen when engageing the Country, the Temeraire was boarded by accident or design by a French Ship on one Side and a Spaniard on the other, the Contest was Vigorous but in the combin'd Ensigns where torn from the Poop and the British hoisted in their Stead.

ABOVE Cartoon showing the British defeating the French and Spanish forces at the Battle of Trafalgar 21 October 1805.

OPPOSITE Hoppner's portrait of Nelson.

loss of Pitt himself. In his second administration, the Prime Minister was less certain of the King's support than formerly. The government was disgraced by the successful impeachment of Pitt's friend, the Earl of Melville, on charges of misappropriating public funds. The Prime Minister was famous for his icy calm but, when he announced Melville's expulsion from the Privy Council, he could not keep back the tears. Disheartened by the King's refusal to sanction negotiations with Fox after Sidmouth's resignation, Pitt began to drink excessively.

The war on the Continent was going badly and the defeat of the Russian and Austrian armies at Austerlitz made Napoleon master of Europe. French success meant the failure of Pitt's life

work. He pointed to a map of Europe hanging on a wall in his sister's house and said 'Roll up that map, it will not be wanted these ten years.' He was only one year too pessimistic. He died on 23 January 1806 in a small rented house facing the luxurious Lodge at Richmond which the King had given to Addington. Pitt was only forty-six at his death, but he had been Prime Minister for nineteen years; he was by far the ablest of George's premiers.

Pitt's death made the King appreciate the worth of a man whom he had come to take too much for granted. The strongest bulwark against those who wanted to reduce the Sovereign's role in government had disappeared. For two days the King was so upset that he would not even admit Ministers wishing to see him on urgent matters of State. Fond as he was of Sidmouth and Eldon, he knew that they had not a quarter of Pitt's talent. When Lord Hawkesbury declined to form a government, George had no choice but to turn to the men from whom Pitt had rescued him so long ago. In his last four years of sanity, the King was more exposed politically than at any time since 1784.

It might have been worse. Lord Grenville, youngest son of George Grenville, formed a coalition government which included some of Pitt's supporters, but the King had to accept Fox as Foreign Secretary. Several of the junior Ministers made it clear that their first loyalty was to the Prince of Wales rather than to his father. Despite earlier enormities, the King assured Fox that the past would be forgotten. The new Foreign Secretary still knew how to act the courtier; whatever he may have said about the French Revolution, he was fundamentally an aristocrat of the old school. In opposition he may have been a wild libertine but, once in office, he showed a devotion to duty and mastery of detail which would not have disgraced Pitt. Privately, George said that Fox's despatches were better written and more lucid than any others in the whole of his reign. The King appreciated his old enemy's changed behaviour and contrasted it with that of his colleagues 'who walked up to me in the way I should have expected from Bonaparte after the battle of Austerlitz'. But Fox's reform did not make up for the loss of Eldon. When the Chancellor went to Buckingham House to give up his seals, the King told him to put them on the sofa; he could not bring himself to take them from his friend's hands.

George feared the new government would revive the Catholic Emancipation issue. Fox had described Pitt's conduct in sacrificing the national interest to the King's prejudice as infamous. The Grenville government was a coalition containing a wide range of opinions. Soon after Fox became Foreign Secretary, he told the Austrian ambassador that there was no point in annoying the King by raising the matter again. Fox wanted to reverse Pitt's policy and come to terms with France; negotiations were opened but the Foreign Secretary was faced with the same conclusion his rival had always insisted on. Napoleon was simply too grasping and too untrustworthy for it to be worthwhile entering into serious discussions.

The King still worried about Fox but he did not have long to speculate about the new Foreign Secretary's intentions. In the summer of 1806 Fox developed dropsy. The Prince of Wales, who did have a streak of kindness, went to see his friend almost every day. Fox died at Chiswick on 13 September 1806, aged fifty-seven. He had survived Pitt by only eight months. Well might Francis Horner declare 'The giant race is extinct and we are left in the hands of little ones, whom we know to be diminutive having measured them against the others.'

It was not to be expected that the King would be as upset at Fox's death as he had been at Pitt's. Fox's nephew, Lord Holland, said that George could scarcely conceal his 'indecent exultation'. This seems unlikely. The King told Sidmouth he genuinely regretted Fox's death; his abilities were badly needed. He was succeeded as Foreign Secretary by Lord Howick, in later life Lord Grey of the Reform Bill.

In some ways, the approach of blindness was a good thing in that it prevented the King working too hard. He had more rest and was always in bed by eleven. He took a little more food and drink, a change which certainly did him no harm. George had separate apartments prepared for himself in the north side of Windsor Castle with furnishings chosen by Princess Elizabeth. The Castle was seriously in need of repair and a start was made under the direction of James Wyatt who did much to revive interest in medieval architecture. The more extravagant new buildings at Windsor were not begun until the Regency. Despite the repairs, it was later discovered that the beam above George III's bed was utterly rotten and could have fallen, bringing tons

'The giant race is extinct and we are left in the hands of little ones'

of masonry on top of him, at any moment.

On the Catholic Question, Lord Grenville knew that he could not win in a head-on clash with the King. His policy was to introduce minor concessions and gradually advance towards his goal. In Irish regiments it was already possible for Catholics to take the rank of Colonel; the Prime Minister proposed that the same provision should apply in English and Scots units. Although George recognised a 'thin edge of the wedge' tactic when he saw one, he realised that it would be difficult to take a stand on a technical point. Reluctantly, he agreed. Unfortunately the pro-Catholic section of the Cabinet overplayed their hand. They framed a Bill which went far beyond the changes the King had accepted and abolished all religious tests at every level of the Army and Navy. The government did not inform George of their new policy but sent the Bill in a batch of miscellaneous documents which were labelled as being of little importance. As George's sight was failing rapidly, it is not surprising that he did not bother to read a document which he had been led to believe was of no consequence. Whatever one may think of Grenville's ends, his means were utterly dishonourable.

Ministers who thought they were dealing with a senile old fool who could be deceived easily were soon taught they had been wrong. Despite the King's protests, Lord Howick persisted in introducing the Bill into Parliament as if George had agreed to it. For a few days the King kept quiet whilst the Bill's supporters blandly assumed that he had become 'insensible to what is passing'. In fact, George was planning another political *coup*. He hurried from Windsor to London to inform the Prime Minister that he would never consent to the Bill. Grenville said that he would withdraw the measure for the time being but would give no promise not to reintroduce it. George had forced Pitt and Fox to bow to his wishes and had no intention of being intimidated by much lesser men. He took the offensive and demanded that the government formally renounce its policy. George took Grenville's refusal calmly and told the Prime Minister 'Then I must look about me.' The Ministry of All Talents was at an end. The Whigs were horrified; after long exclusion from power they had tasted the delights of office for little over a year before being hurled back into the political wilderness. They were to remain there for another twenty-three years. They did not know who to blame more, Grenville or the King.

George's action was daring for a blind man of sixty-eight, but, in fact, the *coup* was accomplished more smoothly and with less reference to constitutional theory than the dismissal of Fox in 1783. The King summoned Eldon and said that he had had no alternative; the responsibility was entirely his and he had consulted no one in reaching his decision. Eldon thought he had never seen the King more collected, composed and cheerful. George still had to create a new government and see it had a majority; few thought he would succeed. Eldon estimated that the new Cabinet would last a fortnight, Lord Hardwicke predicted a general insurrection in Ireland and Lord Howick raised the old cry of 'secret influence behind the Throne'. George assured Sidmouth 'all will come right yet'. The King had more experience than any of his politicians and knew that 'The Church in Danger' was a far more potent slogan than anything Howick had to offer. Addresses of thanks for the King's defence of the Protestant religion came in from all parts of the country. Under the circumstances, the Duke of Portland had little difficulty in constructing a ministry with Eldon back on the Woolsack and most places in the Cabinet filled by pupils of Pitt.

The success in getting rid of Grenville and Howick must have been one of George's last real pleasures. After that sorrows, private and national, came thick and fast. There were deaths of old friends like Bishop Hurd – 'more naturally polite than any man I have ever met with' – the news of the disastrous retreat from Corunna and the disgrace of the Duke of York. After a short period of rebellion, the Duke had shown himself to be one of the most loyal of the King's sons. He had been adequate, if not very inspiring, in his role as Commander-in-Chief. On 27 January 1809 Colonel Wardle, member for Oakhampton, accused the Duke of corruption. Wardle claimed that between 1803 and 1806 the Commander-in-Chief had allowed his mistress, Mary Anne Clarke, to sell commissions and had himself taken a rake-off from the transactions. Promotion in the army was by 'purchase' but the money was paid either to the officer who was retiring or, in the case of a new post, into regimental funds. Now it seemed extra payments were necessary.

The King was indignant at the charges and convinced of his

The British Museum

The British Museum was called into being by the death of Sir Hans Sloane in 1753. He left his collection of manuscripts, books and curiosities to over seventy trustees to create a museum. Montague House in Bloomsbury was purchased to house the collection, and was opened to the public in 1759. George II gave his royal library to the Museum, and his grandson, George III, presented many pieces related to the Civil War. George possessed one of the finest collections of books in England, and the Museum was given these in 1823 by George IV. The collection totalled 65,000 volumes and 868 boxes of pamphlets, and these now form the bulk of the King's Library in the Museum.

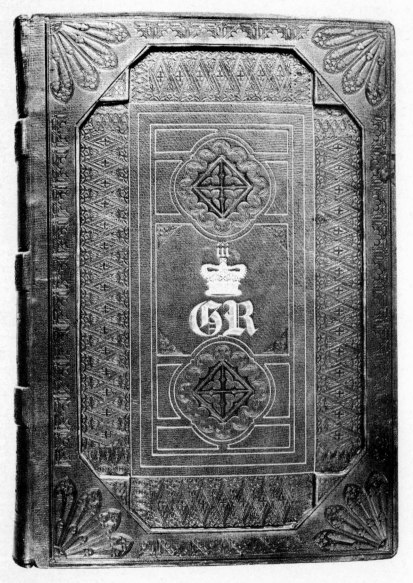

LEFT Brown binding made by the Buckingham Palace Bindery for George III, c. 1815. This volume now belongs to the King's Library in the British Museum.

RIGHT The main staircase in the Museum at Montague House at the beginning of the nineteenth century.

208

son's innocence. Unwisely, he agreed to a public enquiry. In the course of the enquiry, scurrilous details of the Duke's relationship with Mrs Clarke were revealed to a scandal-hungry press. Opinion was less indulgent to immorality in high places than it had been forty years earlier. The King's own high standards had been partly responsible for the change. To make matters worse, the Prince of Wales gave discreet assistance to the hue and cry against his brother. He may have been motivated by malice, but it is more likely that he simply wished to divert attention from his own misdeeds. In vain, the King urged him to rally to the family honour. As the enquiry proceeded, it emerged that Mrs Clarke had conducted a lucrative trade not only in army appointments but also in other departments of State. Although the Duke was shown to have taken no money himself, he had no option but to resign.

The rest of the year was no better: an expedition to the Scheldt failed miserably, and two of the King's daughters became seriously ill. When the Prime Minister was almost completely incapacitated by a stroke, it seemed that the government would collapse and the Whigs return in triumph. George was in despair. He implored Eldon 'For God's sake, don't run away from me!; don't reduce me to the state in which you formerly left me.' The new Premier, Spencer Perceval, proposed a coalition with Grenville. The King was extremely agitated and Eldon feared for his sanity. Fortunately, the negotiations failed and the administration continued with better success than anticipated.

The next year brought even more domestic troubles. The official line was that an attempt had been made to murder the King's son, the Duke of Cumberland, in the early hours of 31 May 1810. The Duke claimed to have beaten off an assassin who was armed with a sharp sword. Soon afterwards, the Duke's page, Sellis, was found with his throat cut. Sellis was left-handed but, at the inquest, it was proved that the wound must have been inflicted by a right-handed person. Rather surprisingly, the jury decided that Sellis had committed suicide after trying to murder his master. The poor man certainly had reason to hate the Duke. He was a Roman Catholic and Cumberland was always making crude jokes about his religion. Unimpeachable witnesses were ready to declare that the Duke

'Don't reduce me to the state in which you formerly left me'

frequently kicked his servants in the presence of guests.

That was bad enough but there was worse to come. The suicide verdict was unconvincing and it was soon common gossip that Sellis had been murdered. The obvious explanation was that Cumberland had faked the attack on himself – he suffered only a very superficial wound – and then murdered his page before raising the alarm. Some thought that Cumberland was subject to fits of insanity, but there were hints that Sellis had to be disposed of because he had discovered that the Duke was a practising homosexual. It is hard to know the truth of the matter but the very existence of such unsavoury rumours cannot have added to George's peace of mind.

That summer, the King had to witness the lingering and painful illness of his favourite daughter, Amelia. It was clear that she would not recover. The King was distressed but still his will-power kept him going. He got up even earlier, usually at six, and went to chapel every morning. He was able to recite the Psalms from memory as accurately as if he had had a prayer book in front of him. At seven in the evening he would appear on the terrace at Windsor, dressed in a blue great-coat, white trousers and a special hat to shield his eyes. One of his last public appearances was on 25 October 1810, when he came out to listen to the bands playing for the fiftieth anniversary of his accession. He was old; he was respected; he had been a good King. It would have been well for George III and his future reputation had he dropped dead that day.

The King had reigned for fifty years; during that time he had been mad for less than one year. George's widely-accepted image as a contemptible idiot is derived almost entirely from the last ten years of his life. There had been signs of trouble on 25 October. The King's voice became loud and one of the Queen's maids, Miss Knight, described how George's mind seemed freed from anxiety about his daughter.

> He said to me 'You are not uneasy I am sure about Amelia. You are not to be deceived but you know that she is in no danger'. At the same time, he squeezed my hand with such force that I could not help crying out. The Queen, however, dragged him away. When the King was seated, he called to each of his sons separately and said things to them equally sublime and instructive, but, very unlike

what he would have said before so many people had he been conscious of the circumstances. I never did and never will repeat what I then heard.

George persisted in thinking his daughter was well. He declared that Amelia was living in Hanover and that she had been given the secret of eternal youth; in fact the poor woman died on 2 November. In the King's case it seemed that medicine had made some progress. The royal doctors under William Heberden insisted there was no need for 'restraint'; George was not strong enough to be a danger. They were not sorry when Simmons refused to serve, only to have their plans wrecked by Perceval who brought in Dr Robert Willis and his strait jacket on 6 November.

On 11 November the King was well enough to be told of his daughter's death. He said he remembered nothing of the previous week and asked if Amelia's funeral had taken place. When told that it had not, he issued detailed instructions for the service. There was a relapse on 17 November. The King was in pain and his mind wandered; he had sense enough to resist attempts to open a vein to bleed him but he was promptly put in a strait jacket and leeches applied to his temples. On 27 November William Heberden told the Privy Council that he was confident that the King would recover; he could not say when. There was a further deterioration after Christmas but then a steady improvement. Unfortunately, the King was now extremely weak. When Perceval called on 29 January 1811 George was sensible but seemed reluctant to talk about public affairs and gave the impression that he would welcome a Regency. He was seventy-three and exhausted; even if his sanity returned it was doubtful if he could sustain the heavy work-load imposed by the Crown. Now that he had time on his hands, George toyed with various pet projects – plans for the rebuilding of Kensington Palace and a scheme for a special order of decoration for women who had done valuable work for the nation. The doctors were appalled by this manifest insanity, 'inconsistent with the dictates of a sound and deliberate judgement'.

It was agreed that a Regency Act should follow Pitt's proposals in 1789 and that the powers would lapse after one year. As this was the first time that the Prince of Wales had actually secured any special authority, Whig hopes of office rose again.

OPPOSITE Portrait of the King at Windsor, as an old and insane man.

On 3 February 1811 the opposition leaders received a curt note from the Prince that he had decided not to change his father's Ministers. In fact, the Regent's views on Catholic Emancipation were identical to those held by George III. The Whigs never understood that they were regarded as a convenient weapon in a family quarrel. When they discovered they had been deceived, men like Grey never forgave the Regent. It had been such a long time since there had been a change of monarch that they had forgotten what usually happened. George III's own case had been an exception. Although a new reign frequently brought changes, these were often less than expected. Princes of Wales tend to become more like their predecessors once they have real responsibility; the Regent was no exception.

As ever, there were wide differences between the King's doctors. One school, led by Heberden, thought there should be only the minimum restraint; the King should be allowed to 'find his own level'. The other, headed by Robert Willis, believed that the only way to erase the King's fantasies was to punish him every time he expressed them. Heberden argued that George must be given something to occupy his mind and that unless this was done, the fantasies would remain. In the spring of 1811 it seemed that Heberden had the upper hand. The King was allowed to arrange concerts and, on Monday 21 May, he made his last appearance in public. Windsor was in great excitement. George appeared steady on his horse as he was led through the Little Park. Church bells rang and guns were fired in his honour. He was out for just under an hour. He was never seen again outside the castle walls.

Queen Charlotte did not trust Heberden and, when George had a slight relapse, she returned to Robert Willis and his all too familiar treatment. The deterioration continued. The King was in pain and, from July 1811, his conversation was incoherent and often obscene. He predicted that his doctors would suddenly sink into Hell, he declared himself immortal and capable of raising men from the dead. There were images recurring from 1788; again he insisted that there had been a great flood, but this time he forgot about his manuscripts and made plans to escape to Denmark. Heberden protested at the treatment the King was subjected to, but the only result was that Robert Willis was joined by his brother John. Even attempts to interest the King by reading aloud from a newspaper were sharply reproved.

After the experimental year, the Regency was made permanent. Thereafter, there were few bulletins and society – but not the people – almost forgot their King. Sometimes, George spoke for twenty-four hours without pausing. The disease seemed to fluctuate in cycles of about eight weeks. Doctors gave up hope of recovery in January 1812 and in June the Queen visited her husband for the last time. The only consolation was that the King's fantasies became more agreeable; he believed himself constantly talking with angels.

Occasional spells of rationality were perhaps more painful than madness. Even the Prince of Wales was reduced to tears when one bright summer morning he found his father lamenting his blindness and reciting verses from Milton's *Samson Agonistes*. In such moods George said he wished to die rather than continue his terrible half life. For most of the time he could not follow the news. In the outside world great things were happening. Spencer Perceval was assassinated in the lobby of the House of Commons; the tide was turning against Napoleon, and Wellington advanced through Spain. Fortunately, George enjoyed a brief recovery in 1814 when he was told of the allied victories. Above all, he was delighted to hear that Hanover had been regained. He may have lost America, but he did not have to surrender his family's homeland. His work and the work of William Pitt had not been in vain.

The recovery did not last long. George must have made a strange and pathetic sight – his hearing gone, his shoulders bent, his eyes blind and staring. He was an old man with wispy white hair and a long silver beard, wearing a violet dressing-gown and shambling around the rooms occupied by Charles I on his way to his trial and execution. George still wore the Garter Star on his chest; although he was senile and insane, he never forgot for an instant that he was King of England.

Like her husband, Queen Charlotte was growing old. She tried to continue George's customs, attending Ascot races in 1816 and the Eton Montem in 1817. On 7 April 1818 she was present at the marriage of her daughter Elizabeth to the Hereditary Prince of Hesse-Homburg. She wore a miniature of the King at the wedding. The Queen died after a painful illness on 17 November 1818, aged seventy-four. Thereafter the Duke of York was entrusted with the care of his father.

The last three years of George's life were practically blank. Sometimes he would get up and strike a few chords on his harpsichord but that was all. If he had a world to live in, it was completely hidden from those around him. He never knew of the deaths of his wife, his son, the Duke of Kent, and his grand-daughter, Princess Charlotte. The King had his last attack at Christmas 1819. He was sleepless and spoke nonsense for fifty-eight hours; then he sank into a coma; he died at 8.32 pm on 29 January 1820, aged eighty-one years and eight months.

George was buried at night on 16 February. A long torchlight procession moved to St George's Chapel. The coffin entered and the choir sang 'I know that my Redeemer liveth'. As the body was lowered into the vault, the Garter King at Arms proclaimed the titles of the dead Sovereign. In many ways the whole of George's life was tinged with sadness. He was unfortunate in most of his relations and cursed by a disease which his doctors treated with torture. The country was more fortunate in its King. His mind was limited but he held fast to what he believed was right, the honour of England and its Crown. It is hard to think of better values for bringing the country through sixty years of change and danger.

Select bibliography

Butterfield, Sir Herbert, *George III and the Historians* (1957)
  George III, Lord North and the People, (1949)
Foord, A. S., *His Majesty's Opposition, 1714-1830* (1964)
Macalpine, I., and Hunter, R., *George III and the Mad Business* (1969)
Marshall, Dorothy, *Eighteenth Century England* (1962)
Mathias, P., *The First Industrial Nation* (1969)
Pares, R., *George III and the Politicians* (1953)
Rudé, George, *Hanoverian London* (1971)
Trevelyan, G. M., *Illustrated Social History*, vol III (1942)

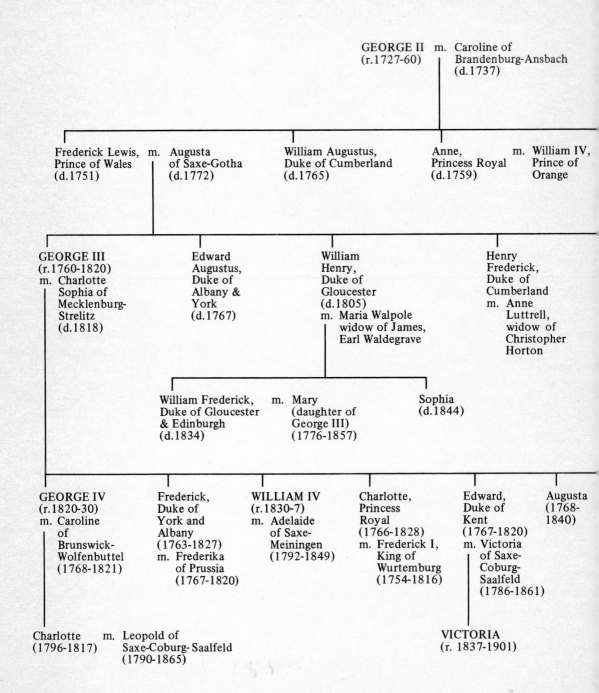

GEORGE II   m.   Caroline of
(r.1727-60)   Brandenburg-Ansbach
           (d.1737)

Frederick Lewis,   m.   Augusta   William Augustus,   Anne,   m.   William IV,
Prince of Wales   of Saxe-Gotha   Duke of Cumberland   Princess Royal   Prince of
(d.1751)   (d.1772)   (d.1765)   (d.1759)   Orange

GEORGE III   Edward   William   Henry
(r.1760-1820)   Augustus,   Henry,   Frederick,
m. Charlotte   Duke of   Duke of   Duke of
   Sophia of   Albany &   Gloucester   Cumberland
   Mecklenburg-   York   (d.1805)   m. Anne
   Strelitz   (d.1767)   m. Maria Walpole   Luttrell,
   (d.1818)   widow of James,   widow of
                                Earl Waldegrave   Christopher
                                                   Horton

William Frederick,   m.   Mary   Sophia
Duke of Gloucester   (daughter of   (d.1844)
& Edinburgh   George III)
(d.1834)   (1776-1857)

GEORGE IV   Frederick,   WILLIAM IV   Charlotte,   Edward,   Augusta
(r.1820-30)   Duke of   (r.1830-7)   Princess   Duke of   (1768-
m. Caroline   York and   m. Adelaide   Royal   Kent   1840)
   of   Albany   of Saxe-   (1766-1828)   (1767-1820)
   Brunswick-   (1763-1827)   Meiningen   m. Frederick I,   m. Victoria
   Wolfenbuttel   m. Frederika   (1792-1849)   King of   of Saxe-
   (1768-1821)   of Prussia   Wurtemburg   Coburg-
                 (1767-1820)   (1754-1816)   Saalfeld
                                                          (1786-1861)

Charlotte   m.   Leopold of   VICTORIA
(1796-1817)   Saxe-Coburg- Saalfeld   (r. 1837-1901)
               (1790-1865)

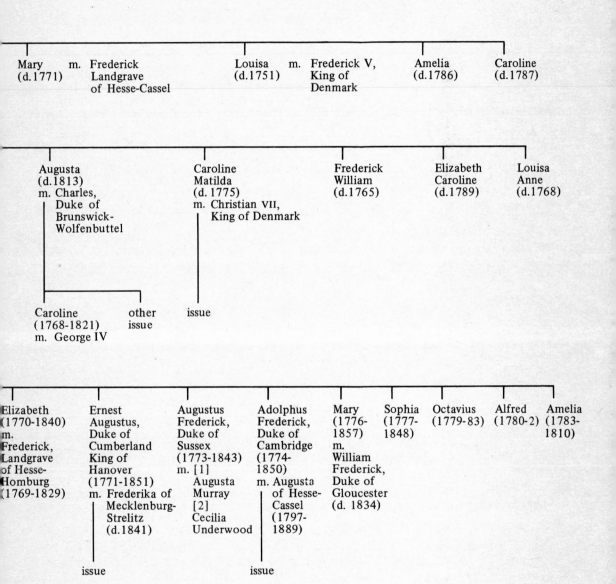

Mary (d.1771)   m.   Frederick Landgrave of Hesse-Cassel

Louisa (d.1751)   m.   Frederick V, King of Denmark

Amelia (d.1786)

Caroline (d.1787)

Augusta (d.1813) m. Charles, Duke of Brunswick-Wolfenbuttel

Caroline Matilda (d.1775) m. Christian VII, King of Denmark

Frederick William (d.1765)

Elizabeth Caroline (d.1789)

Louisa Anne (d.1768)

Caroline (1768-1821) m. George IV

other issue

issue

Elizabeth (1770-1840) m. Frederick, Landgrave of Hesse-Homburg (1769-1829)

Ernest Augustus, Duke of Cumberland King of Hanover (1771-1851) m. Frederika of Mecklenburg-Strelitz (d.1841)

Augustus Frederick, Duke of Sussex (1773-1843) m. [1] Augusta Murray [2] Cecilia Underwood

Adolphus Frederick, Duke of Cambridge (1774-1850) m. Augusta of Hesse-Cassel (1797-1889)

Mary (1776-1857) m. William Frederick, Duke of Gloucester (d. 1834)

Sophia (1777-1848)

Octavius (1779-83)

Alfred (1780-2)

Amelia (1783-1810)

issue

issue

219

Index